EVERYDAY TAROT

using the cards to make better life decisions

GAIL FAIRFIELD

WEISERBOOKS
Boston, MA/York Beach, ME

First published in 2002 by
Red Wheel/Weiser, LLC
368 Congress Street
Boston, MA 02210
www.redwheelweiser.com

Cataloging-in-Publication Data
Fairfield, Gail.
    Everyday Tarot / Gail Fairfield.
        p. cm.
    Originally published: 5th ed. Smithville, IN : Ramp Creek, 1990.
    Includes index.
    ISBN 978-1-57863-268-8
    1. Tarot. I. Title.
    BF1879.T2F35   1997
    133.3'2424--dc21   96-54821
                                                                    CIP

Printed in Canada

TCP

09 08 07 06 05 04 03 02
8 7 6 5 4 3 2 1

The paper used in this publication meets the minimum requirements of the
American National Standard for Information Sciences—Permanence of Paper for
Printed Library Materials Z39.48-1992 (R 1997).

ACKNOWLEDGMENTS

In its many forms and revisions, this book would not have been possible without the
assistance, expertise, and support of Kay Ries, Betty and John Fairfield, Barbara and
Tony Frederick, Judith Pendleton, Cherry Johnson, Francine Carroll, Candy Cruea,
Ruth Hopper, Debra Clark, and all my clients and students. Thank you all!

TABLE OF CONTENTS

FOREWORD

Gail Fairfield's *Choice-Centered Tarot* is a fine addition to the expanding body of literature on these mysterious ancient cards, which many are finding to be highly relevant and useful tools for 20th century explorers of consciousness. Her book wisely emphasizes the psychological meanings of the Tarot, showing in clear and simple fashion how the card symbols, which at first seem so strange and perplexing, can yield powerful insights, and help people come to greater self-understanding and the ability to make creative and responsible choices in all kinds of life situations.

The set of mythic images which constitutes the Tarot has exercised a singular fascination on the minds and feelings of countless men and women, particularly those who are consciously searching for a way of self-knowledge or self-transformation. The emotional resonance and mental interest, which the Tarot tends to induce, seem to be in no way diminished by the fact that all attempts to definitely establish its origin or history have been amazingly unsuccessful. Thus the Tarot presents itself to us as a kind of phenomenon, an unexplained message in the form of images of obscure origin, that somehow have the power to challenge and stimulate our deepest intuitions, awakening echoes in long-buried strata of the psyche. Like the Sphinx, or like the *I Ching*, or like much ancient mythology, the Tarot poses a kind of riddle, at first without apparent meaning. Since no conceptual interpretations come along with these ancient symbolic structures, we are forced to rely on our own inner knowing, our own inner response, in order to understand the meaning.

The Tarot apparently made its first recorded appearance in Europe in the Middle Ages, as a deck of cards used in games of chance and also by fortune-tellers for divination. Some have attributed it to the Gypsies; others have argued that it was already in existence long before the Gypsies first arrived in Europe. Writers on occult history and philosophy have propounded theories of an Egyptian, or Indian, or Arabic origin, or even Atlantean. Unfortunately (or perhaps appropriately) none of these theories for an ancient origin of the Tarot has any scholarly or scientific evidence to support it. So we are left with a set of symbols that carry meaning for people, even though the "real" or "original" meanings may be lost for ever.

As a device for not only predicting the future, i.e. fortune-telling, but also for providing insight and symbolic tools for self-understanding, the Tarot stands in the company of other divinatory systems, such as the *I Ching*, numerology, astrology, rune-casting, bone-games and others. These systems have somehow incorporated teachings of deep psychological wisdom into the structure of a game, or a fortune-telling ritual. Some writers have even suggested that in the case of the Tarot, attaching the inner teachings to a card-game, was a deliberate strategy designed to maximize the survival of those teachings. Ancient sages, according to this view, apparently felt that humanity's thirst for knowledge and wisdom was subject to considerable decay over time, but the desire to predict the future and control one's fate was deemed a much more suitable trait. And thus we have card games, and fairy tales, and stick counting games, that have preserved deep inner meanings, accessible to those who can decipher them.

For example, the symbolism of the four elements, which is a very ancient archetypal pattern with both psychological and cosmic meanings, is central to the understanding of astrology, alchemy and many shamanic practices, and is embedded in the Tarot in the form of the four suits (swords, wands, cups and pentacles or discs). These four suits were carried over, in transmuted form, into modern playing cards. And thus our modern playing cards, with their spades, clubs, hearts and diamonds, probably unbeknownst to the majority of players, can relate us back to these ancient archetypes. "Spades" are the descendants of the Tarot "swords," which symbolize the intellectual discrimination, the mental level of consciousness, the element "air;" "wands" in Tarot, which became "clubs" in modern decks, are variously interpreted as perception, intuition, imagination . . . the "fire" element. The Tarot "cups" symbolize the emotional, feeling level of consciousness, . . . associated with the element "water" in other ancient systems, and transformed, appropriately enough, to "hearts" in the modern playing cards; and the Tarot cards' "pentacles" or "discs" or "coins," which became "diamonds" in modern times, is traditionally related to the "earth" element, and thus the material level of reality, including financial and somatic realities. These psychological and elemental symbolisms of the suits become central in the interpretation of Tarot readings or spreads, and the author of the present book makes amply clear. There is of course ample latitude for individual variation and the unique intuitions of each person who uses the Tarot, in interpreting these symbols.

There are some similarities between a Tarot consultation or reading, when it is done for psychological purposes, as laid out in this book, and the projective assessment methods used in psychology, such as the Rorschach and the Thematic Apperception Test, or T.A.T. In the latter especially, the client is asked to tell a story in response to an ambiguous picture showing one or more persons in some kind of situation or inter-action. These stories are then interpreted as revealing unconscious inner dynamics of the individual, who is assumed to have "projected" these contents into the story. In the case of the Tarot, the pictures are not interpreted along psychodynamic lines, rather they are given intuitive interpretations based on the traditional meanings of the symbols por-trayed on the cards. However, research done by Arthur Rosengarten for his Ph.D. dissertation at the California Institute of Integral Studies, has shown that Tarot readings can be used to assess various unconscious dynamics, in a fashion quite comparable to, and with comparable validity as, TAT stories and dreams. All three of these were seen, in his work, as methods of "accessing" the unconscious.

C.G. Jung's theory of synchronicity provides a useful framework for understanding the Tarot, as well as other divinatory procedures. According to this view, one would say that in a card reading there is a "meaningful coincidence," or synchronicity, between the symbols on the cards selected, and the person's life situation. For example, a person may draw the Lovers card, when she or he is actually in love at that time. This kind of synchronistic event is facilitated, according to Jung, when an archetype is strongly activated in the individual's unconscious. The symbols on the cards, in so far as they portray deep universal human themes (archetypes), can evoke and facilitate in the questioner or seeker a fresh and meaningful perspective on their life situation.

Ralph Metzner, Ph.D.
San Francisco, Calif.

INTRODUCTION

What is psychic ability? It is simply the ability to use certain tools or mechanisms for tuning in to the cycles and rhythms of the Universe and our lives. Everyone has psychic capability, just as everyone can potentially float in the water. People who have been taught to be afraid of the water, who believe that the water can hurt them, may never choose to learn to float. Similarly, those who have been taught to distrust, discount, or fear psychic processes, may find it difficult to openly accept and explore them. By working through those fears, people can reshape their beliefs and embrace their own psychic potential.

If you really believe that you are not lovable, no one can prove to you that you are. You'll set it up, over and over again, to prove to yourself that no one could possibly care about you. No matter what loving things people say or do, you'll discount them. You'll tell yourself that they can't possibly know what they're talking about and that their judgment can't be trusted. You'll continue to reinforce the belief that you're not lovable. If you begin to believe that you might be lovable, that at least you could like your self a little, you'll find that others begin to respond to you more positively. Amazingly enough, you'll soon find that you're becoming more and more lovable.

If you believe that you're not psychic, the same process holds true. No matter what happens, you'll dismiss it as coincidence, happenstance, or a trick. If you believe that you can't be psychic, you won't be psychic. If, on the other hand, you believe that you could be psychic, little things will begin to open up for you. You will get "hunches" and you might know who's calling before you answer the phone. You'll begin to remember some of your dreams and realize that they hold messages for you. You may even begin to explore some of the more traditional fields of psychic study.

Any psychic study involves learning to use certain tools. These tools are like shovels, hammers, and circular saws. They have potential. We can use them if we know how, or we can let their potential sit unused. The purpose of learning how to use a tool is to get some kind of result from it. When you learn to repair and run a rototiller, your purpose is to make the tiller useful, to set it up to plow a garden space. You may enjoy the repair process and really love the way the parts fit together so beautifully. But, much as you enjoy working with the tool, the ultimate objective is still to use it to plow the soil. Only then can the seeds be planted so the flowers and vegetables can grow. Psychic tools, also, are only valuable if they are useful and applicable to our lives. When we set out to develop a psychic skill, the skill is not an end in itself. It is the means to an end; it is the pathway to the garden.

The question becomes, "How do I know if a tool is useful to me?" First of all, the tool needs to feel comfortable to you. If you love spading and hate the noise of a rototiller, a spade is a better tool for you. If you love the visual symbolism of the Tarot cards, while the math of Astrology overwhelms you, maybe the Tarot is right for you. Or, maybe you are interested in learning to use a variety of tools so that you can pick the best tool or combination of tools for each situation. It takes a long time to spade an acre garden; in that case you might want to go back to the rototiller. Within one field, a particular approach, like a particular shovel, may feel most comfortable.

Once you've found a psychic tool that appeals to you, its usefulness will depend on how much insight you can gain from it. If it's an effective tool for you, it will heighten your awareness and perception and give you a new perspective on your own personal reality. It will help you see how you can work most creatively with your life to set up the reality you want.

Like a hot air balloon, your psychic tool can lift you out of your everyday reality and give you a new point of view on things. Imagine that a balloon could take you outside of time. You could then see the whole panorama of your life spread out below you. From the balloon level, you could see all the people, issues, events, stresses, and joys of your life. You might even see some of your other lives. You could see how all the factors of your lives mesh together to create your past, present, and future.

As you look at the panorama of the future, you can see all the multiple possibilities of directions in which you could go. You can see how some of the factors in your present reality tend to lead toward one or another future direction. You can even see how you are actively pursuing one of those futures. You can see that by making certain choices and adjustments in the present, you could change the probable future. A different future could come more clearly into focus as a strong possibility.

As you look at your past, you notice all the details of it. You recognize that you've only been remembering one small part of the past, only using a few of your memories as a foundation for your present experiences. You realize that you can again make some choices. You can choose to remember and focus on parts of the past that you've avoided or ignored. You can effectively create a new emphasis in your past and restructure what the past means to you. By restructuring or re-remembering the past, you create a different perception of the present. By seeing all the potential of the future, you recognize your full power and claim the freedom to create the future that you want. You see what you need to do in the present in order to create that adjusted past and future.

For example, imagine you're an artist, a painter, and you had an accident last year that caused you to lose your painting arm. In looking at the future, you can see how you could become bitter about the loss of your arm. You can see yourself feeling helpless and hopeless and relying more and more on others to support you. The more others help you, the more dependent you become and the worse you feel about yourself. You begin feeling as though you are no good, you have no skills to offer, you can't create anymore. At present, that is the future that you are creating. You're doing things right now, in the present, to create that dismal future.

You look to the past and, at first, all you can see is the accident. Your whole past seems full of this accident because it looms so large in your memory. This seems to be "the" important thing that has affected your life. Then you start seeing the other parts of your past. You notice your writing and speaking ability. You see all your friends. You remember your love and appreciation of music. You see all the things you've always done with your other arm. You begin to realize that you have other creative avenues open to you. First of all, you can learn to paint with your other arm. You can teach, dictate articles, and speak about painting. You can develop your ability as a music critic. You can spend time with the people you love. All of a sudden, your life is full of ways to creatively express yourself. You realize that by exploring those avenues, you are making choices that change the probable direction of the future. Instead of helplessness and dependence, you have strength and self-respect. You have productive and supportive interactions with others.

This is why re-remembering history is so important in liberation movements. Women, gay people, differently able people, working class people, and people of color have been shown only the past that is reflected in white, male, middle class, able-bodied, heterosexual history books. Seeing that the whole past is made up of this group, we could find it hard to see anything of value in our own lives. When we actually start digging around in our memories of the past, we find all kinds of different facts. New things come into focus and the history book past becomes less prominent and less important.

As women, we've learned that there have been strong, independent women throughout history who have been creative inventors, leaders, pioneers, and just plain survivors. We find out that other women have been through abuse, disaster and divorce, boredom, self-hate, and put-downs. Other women have felt that they were helpless and useless. Other women have come through those experiences and feelings and established new levels of strength and self-respect. Reclaiming and rediscovering the past, knowing that many women have survived and made strong contributions to the world, helps us to make creative choices about our lives. We recognize that women do have the power and ability to shape events and affect the world. Our newly remembered herstory affects our futures.

Similarly, as gay people, people of color, or differently able people, we are discovering that history is full of people like us, if we would only re-remember history. We are connected with a rich, varied past, not just the past that one group chooses to remember. The fullness of our own pasts gives us a lot to work with when we are creating the futures we want to have.

Any psychic tool should function as the hot air balloon that allows you to see your past, present and futures. It ought to give you new analyses and perceptions about the past. It needs to, literally, put the events of the past in the proper perspective. Once it gives you that new and solid foundation, your tool needs to show you the choices that are available to you. It needs to give you insight into the adjustments you can make in the present, to create the future that you want. Just as you can learn to fly a hot air balloon, you can study and practice using your psychic tools. Or you may choose to find someone else to fly your balloon for you — a psychic reader can pilot you up in the air so that you can get a good view of your life. You may even choose to be a pilot, a reader, for others. But always remember that the purpose of the flight is to get a panoramic view, an insight into the possibilities.

There is a difference between insight and prediction. A predictive use of psychic tools shows you primarily the past and future that loom the largest on the horizon. It tells you your probable direction. Making a prediction is like calculating the odds of your balloon hitting a tree, based on the past movements of the balloon and the forces acting on it at present. If the odds are high enough, the prediction says "you will hit that tree." Any psychic prediction is a probability, based on the past that is most intensely remembered and the situations and events that are at work in the present.

When a psychic tool is used for insight, it can give you all kinds of information about the past, present and future. You may see your probable direction, but you can also see some possible alternatives. These options give you the choices of landing or redirecting your balloon before you hit the tree! Your insights can help you recognize the factors in your present situation that tend to support various futures. The choices are then up to you. You are in charge of your life, not dependent on someone or something else to make your decisions for you. With new insight, you can re-create the past, re-structure the present, and re-align the future. Through reading this book, you can learn how to use the Tarot cards as an insightful psychic tool.

1

CHOOSING A TAROT DECK

The key to the Tarot is in the symbols used on the cards. They are the triggers and catalysts for our insights into ourselves and our lives. These symbols are chosen and drawn by people who are depicting the Tarot concepts in ways that are comfortable for them. Since an author's insights are filtered through her personal system of beliefs, her work will be affected by her psychological characteristics, philosophy of life, cultural values, and experiences with the Tarot. Since the older Tarot materials reflect the "truths" of the Middle Ages, our experiences with the Tarot are often colored by the belief systems and values of that era.

If we want to apply the Tarot to our lives, we need to understand the basic concepts that lie beneath the symbols drawn by any given individual. Once we have uncovered these concepts, we can try on the symbols that have been used to represent them. We can decide whether the symbols chosen by a given author for a particular deck of cards are appropriate for us, in our own cultures and subcultures. Through understanding some of the kinds of symbols in use, we can more easily evaluate the Tarot materials that are available and choose the decks that work best for each of us.

HUMAN SYMBOLS

Pictures of people represent, most clearly, the values and attitudes of the people who have drawn them. The images represent somebody's view of people and human interactions. Because we are all people, the human image is perhaps the most powerful of all the symbols used in the Tarot. Whenever we see images of people of certain sizes, colors, genders, and ages, we respond to them according to our own identification with those characteristics. Some of our responses are easily identifiable; others are more subtle. Because of the complexity of our responses to the human image, it is especially important for us to be aware of the impact that these symbols have on us.

Gender As A Symbol

A traditional analysis of human interaction is that which links males with assertiveness, females with nurturing, and their union with wholeness. The union of men and women is supposed to be the ideal whole from which creativity (in the form of children) springs. When this system is being used in Tarot materials, the images of men and women and their interactions can represent very definite personality qualities and conditions. In some traditional texts, a male image on a card immediately indicates a quality of control, command, aggression, or leadership. A female image represents qualities of passivity, nurturing, submission, or receptivity. In this analysis, women who have assertive qualities are seen as going against nature. A traditional text might say something like, "If the querent is a woman, this card shows that she is a shrew and a troublemaker . . . if a man, this card shows that he is strong and commanding." Men who are sensitive are seen as weak. Another text might read "If the querent is a man, this card shows that he is ineffective and not respected . . . if a woman, this card shows that she is strong in wifely qualities." Tarot texts that narrowly attribute some qualities to men and some to women, end up alienating people who want to experience the whole range of human qualities.

In the traditional analysis, there is no way to achieve wholeness except by the union of male with female. Individuals who choose to remain independent are seen as incapable of achieving true fulfillment.

7

Any relationships between members of the same gender are considered innately inferior. In fact, individuals who choose these options are not even represented in most Tarot materials. Our personal growth can be severely limited if we feel that our own energies are not complete or unified unless we are in a relationship with a person of the opposite sex. We each have the potential for wholeness within us. We can be whole persons who choose to interact with other whole persons, of either gender, not people who are searching for completion from outside of ourselves.

Many of us are beginning to see that the qualities of assertiveness and nurturance exist apart from the genders of male and female. The unification of the aggressive, active energy and the supportive, enfolding energy can happen within one individual, not just between individuals. Some Tarot materials are beginning to reflect the changes in our attitudes toward personality qualities and their associations with specific genders. However, many decks and books still reflect the more traditional, rigidly defined sex roles. As we work with various Tarot decks and texts, we need to be aware of the sexist and heterosexist attitudes that they reflect and reinforce. We need to recognize that sex-role stereotyping is not an integral element of a sacred teaching; it is simply the point of view of a person who designed a particular Tarot deck.

Race As A Symbol

Most Tarot decks are blatantly racist in that they confine themselves to the use of Caucasian images. The exclusion of people of other races is significant in itself and reinforces the misconception that the Tarot (which reflects the pattern of life) is only relevant to the white race. Where images of people of color are used, it is important to note what they symbolize. Often, they are supposed to symbolize our fears and pains, our guilt, our unknown depths, our uncontrollable urges, and our bondage or entrapment. For example, in some decks the only Black people are The Devil, slaves, or The Hanged Man. Most often, images of people of color are used to symbolize fearful parts of our lives.

Each individual needs to discover those fears, passions, and doubts within herself and to claim them as common to us all. White people do not have to use images of people of color to symbolize the things

8

they fear and/or want to control within themselves. Also, we need to explore the dominant culture's assumption that "white is better, lighter, brighter, and more positive." When we recognize that all people have creative energy, we do not have to use images of white people to symbolize our enlightened awareness. We need to examine the decks we use to see the ways in which racism is being perpetuated, either by the exclusion of people of color or by their inclusion in negative or violent imagery.

Class As A Symbol

In Europe, throughout the last four or five centuries, the Tarot has been used primarily by the ruling class, occult initiates, educated philosophers, and witches or gypsies. The insights and information of the witches and gypsies has been transmitted by word of mouth and is not always publicly available to us. Instead, we have the materials that have been developed and published by the privileged classes. We can see that bias in the names of the cards and the images on them. The scholars and nobles that developed the Tarot materials as we know them today, depicted Emperors, Kings, and Popes. They drew on esoteric philosophies, mystical teachings, classical works, and the literature, history, and myths of many cultures. They saw the Tarot as a tool to be used by the initiated or privileged people who had the leisure and education to study and understand an intricate maze of symbolism.

Only in the twentieth century has the Tarot become available for use by the general public. Of course, as interest and business have boomed, the number and variety of Tarot materials has increased as well. But in many Twentieth Century materials we still find a focus on the esoteric meaning of the Tarot, as it was analyzed by the rich and educated elite. We find that the old relationships between the rulers and the ruled, the educated and the less educated, are maintained. The interpretations of the cards often equate the power of the upper class position with positive qualities while they associate the lower class situation with negative qualities. The language used in many of the texts is still aimed at the scholar.

Today, we have an opportunity to demystify the Tarot. Some authors are already beginning to present interpretations that steer clear of references to scholarly literature and avoid allusions to obscure mythological or philosophical writings. They are attempting to make the Tarot a tool that is easily available to everyone. Many are even renaming the cards in an attempt to have the titles describe the meanings of the cards instead of reflecting archaic social structures.

By using basic concepts and straightforward language in our work with the Tarot, we can begin to break down the barriers of class and make the Tarot accessible to everyone.

Body Image As A Symbol

Hardly any of us look like Greek Gods or Egyptian Goddesses! Few of us have "perfectly" proportioned bodies (whatever perfect is). Some of us are fatter, some of us are thinner; some of us are taller, some are extra short. Most of us have some kind of physical impairment to our everyday functioning. Some of us wear glasses or move around in wheelchairs. Some of us use hearing aids, some have internal disabilities that no one can see, some are missing limbs. We are all unique in our body shapes and capacities and we are all capable, creative persons. In most Tarot materials, people who are not "ideal" in their physical shape or abilities are only included if they symbolize poverty, disaster, or misfortune. Most Tarot decks don't show us ourselves. They show us somebody's concept of a perfect person. As new Tarot materials emerge out of a broader consciousness, we are beginning to see images of real people in the cards.

Age As A Symbol

Tarot decks generally treat children as creative, energetic beings who are ready to begin life with enthusiasm and faith. Young people are seen as being a bit reckless, willing to take a few risks, but on the road to adventure and experience. Middle-aged people are seen as the sensible and mature leaders of society. Older people are depicted only occasionally; when they are included, they are usually seen as quiet, but inactive, sages. We need to begin including more older people in our Tarot materials. We need images of people of all ages with various energy levels and personality qualities.

As we examine Tarot materials, we must be aware of the value judgments that the author has made when depicting various people. In addition, we can tune into the ways in which the author portrays the interaction between those people. Each of us interacts with other people in our lives. Some of us interact with many people, some interact with only a few. Some of us choose to be involved with people who are like us; some enjoy being with those who are different. But we all interact with other people.

Many of our relationships involve a power imbalance. When two people get together, one person usually has more status, power, or control than the other. When whole groups get together the imbalance of power is most marked. In our world today, men tend to have power over women, whites over people of color, heterosexuals over homosexuals, able-bodied over differently able, mature adult over younger or older people, management over workers, rich over poor, political leaders over followers, educated over less-educated, and so forth. In one way or another, the imbalance of power between individuals and groups has touched each of our lives.

We tend to feel that we have power if we control other people and that we lack power if we are controlled by others. This control involves some individuals or groups setting and enforcing the limits and conditions of other people's growth and development.

There is also another way of looking at power and control. We can gain control over our own lives without controlling the lives of others; others can control their lives without having to control us. We each can have the personal power to be ourselves, individually and in groups, without measuring ourselves against one another. We can take charge of ourselves, make choices based on our own needs, and become responsible to and for ourselves. We do not have to allow or expect one person or group to make decisions for another, to be responsible for another, or to generally take charge of another. Basically, that is what liberation movements are about: groups of people gaining control over their own lives.

Many Tarot materials depict relationships only from the unequal-power perspective. They often associate the dominant, powerful person or group with positive qualities and the powerless group or person with negative qualities. When we look at the Devil card in some decks, we may get the message that the Devil is bad, male, and Black. On the other hand, the Emperor is almost always presented as a white man who is an authority figure. It is encouraging that some of the newer Tarot materials do depict equality-based relationships between groups and individuals and support the development of personal power — the power of self-determination.

It's clear that placing a person on a Tarot card is no simple act. Interpretation of the message of that human image happens on conscious and unconscious levels. We need to look carefully at the cards we choose to use and examine which of our own attitudes they represent and reinforce.

*   *   *   *   *

Now that we have explored the human image as a symbol, let's take a look at some of the other symbol systems that are used in the Tarot:

MYTHOLOGICAL SYMBOLS

The purpose of mythology is to tell a story that explains why things are the way they are: why it rains, why there are poor people, where the sun goes at night, why we feel anger or jealousy, what happens when we die, why winter comes, etc. These stories have the psychological power to make us feel comfortable with the events of our lives. Mythology helps us feel that there is a reason for what happens and shows us where we fit into the picture.

People who design Tarot decks use many of the mythologies of the past and present, including Egyptian, Greek, Oriental, and Mayan mythologies as well as scientific, Biblical, and Matriarchal stories about why things are the way they are. They choose mythologies that represent universal truths to them and use the symbols of those mythologies in their Tarot materials. Some authors do an excellent job of educating us about their chosen mythological symbols. Others leave the research up to the readers and assume that the users of their materials will understand the symbols in the decks. Suffice it to say that mythological symbols from any source are only valuable if we are familiar with them. Once we explore the stories, we may find them to be priceless in helping us to understand our lives or we may find them to be useless. It is up to each of us to choose the mythologies, and Tarot decks, that are appropriate for our lives.

NATURAL SYMBOLS

Images of plants and animals appear in the Tarot quite often. They are usually part of a scene in which people also appear or part of a border, background or stylized pattern. Sometimes they appear in a more central, focal position. Symbols drawn from the weather and the seasons also appear frequently. While some of the symbols for plants, animals and the elements seem to have universal meaning, others are used by authors who intend for them to have very specific meanings. As in the case of mythologies, some authors explain their symbols well; others do not.

Of course the impact of natural images will change depending on a reader's own experience. Snow might have a multitude of meanings for a person raised in Alaska and no meaning at all for someone raised in Panama. Each person's response to the snow, lightning, a dog, or a tree will color her response to the cards that display those symbols.

RELIGIOUS SYMBOLS

Religious symbols are very commonly used in the Tarot. In the more traditional decks, the symbols are usually taken from the Christian tradition (the Cross, angels, priests, the Pope, and saints) or from the Jewish tradition (the Torah and Tree of Life). Deities, revered people, and meaningful motifs from Eastern and Pagan religions are also finding their ways into the Tarot. With the revival of Witchcraft and Goddess-oriented religions, many of the old gods are taking a back seat in our lives and in our newer Tarot decks. However, it is important to remember that religious symbols are just that—symbols that represent important concepts for people who hold particular religious beliefs. Out of context, the symbols may be meaningless. They may even create an adverse reaction if the person using the cards has negative feelings about those religions.

ASTROLOGICAL AND OTHER OCCULT SYMBOLS

The symbols of Astrology and other occult languages are often displayed in Tarot decks. This is because many of these systems are used throughout the world and their symbols do provide a common bond or language among all the people who study the occult. The symbols of Astrology, for example, have become more and more popularized until many people are at least aware that ♋ is an astrological symbol even though they may not be able to name it or interpret its meaning. The yin/yang symbol, I Ching hexagrams, the Egyptian ankh, and other symbols of near-eastern or oriental philosophies are also finding their ways into western life. With a "little education," anyone could use these symbols in their work with the Tarot.

Having access to the "little education" can be a problem. For those who are already familiar with one or more of these philosophies, knowledge of these symbols can add immeasurably to their understanding of the Tarot. However, most people are only vaguely aware of the meaning of these symbols and may not have access to learning about them. Also, learning to use Astrology or the I Ching can be a lifetime study in itself! While such study would certainly enhance your work with the Tarot, it isn't a prerequisite to that work.

LANGUAGE SYMBOLS

Every culture has developed some kind of language and some set of symbols for that language; many Tarot decks use those language symbols. Specific words in Spanish, Hebrew, or English will be quite evocative for those who speak or read those languages. Some language symbols can even be used in cross-cultural ways. In the Hebrew mystical tradition, the study of the Kabbalah, it is said that people can become enlightened through studying the forms of the Hebrew letters. The shapes of the letters are mandalas that anyone can use for meditation. New international languages, such as aUI, have been developed to use the symbolism that lies beneath language and to make a single language alphabet accessible to everyone. Other languages, such as Chinese and Mayan, use pictographs that evoke concepts and elements of nature even though we may not be able to literally interpret the symbols.   Unlike the letters of European alphabets, the characters of more pictorial alphabets have meanings in themselves. Each character portrays a whole concept on its own and contributes to the more complex messages of the words and/or sentences. In the Tarot,

14

these pictorial characters are sometimes presented singly and sometimes presented in groups that form words or images. Readers can interpret them based on their intuitive sense of the meaning of the symbols or based on their knowledge of the language being used.

For some people who are fascinated by languages, a Tarot system that is full of characters and letters and words may provide a wonderful jumping-off place for discovery and exploration. For others, too many language symbols will be distracting and confusing.

MUSIC SYMBOLS

Musical tones are definitely cross-cultural. Each person has an intuitive and emotional reaction to sound and/or vibration. The study of correspondences between musical tones and the Tarot has just begun. Perhaps, someday, musical pieces will be written about each Tarot card and people will come to understand the cards through their own emotional reactions to the sounds. How to symbolize those sounds on cards, in an easily decipherable way, would still be a challenge—not everyone reads or hears music.

COLOR SYMBOLS

Many Tarot decks have been produced which use color quite effectively. There is no question that color, like music, evokes a strong response in people of any cultural background. Even those with visual impairment have emotional reactions to color. It is probable that our feelings are impacted by our cultural patterning and training. In the West, for example, black or dark colors are frequently viewed through racist filters and seen as negative. Many cultures use color in their folk arts in specific and defined ways. Most of us do choose Tarot decks with colors that we find to be personally appealing though we may be unaware of the reasons behind our preferences. Many authors explain the color "coding" used in their decks making it easier for us to understand their intentions whether or not we agree with them! Color adds so much to the Tarot that it's important for us to be consciously aware of its emotional, political, and esthetic power.

NUMBER SYMBOLS

Another concept that is very cross-cultural is that of number. When a child puts a few stones together on a leaf, or arranges some sticks in groupings, she may not know that she has three stones or eight sticks or that those numbers have names. But, she does have an intuitive understanding of the groupings of more-ness and not-as-much-ness. Every culture has developed a system of number, based on counting objects. While not everyone uses the same name for "three" or the same symbols (3 or III or •••), everyone recognizes the quality of "three-ness" in a grouping of three sticks, stones, or bumps. Translating number concepts into various languages can easily be done by using the number of objects on a card. We can use three dots on a braille card, for instance, instead of the numeral 3. Number is a powerful symbolic system that can be used by people who have no opportunity or desire to learn another system or language before they approach the Tarot.

*   *   *   *   *

To return to the initial question of this chapter: how do you choose the Tarot deck that is right for you? As you examine Tarot decks, be aware of the symbols in them because these symbols do represent powerful concepts. Determine for yourself which attitudes these concepts trigger within you, on both conscious and subconscious levels. Recognize the beliefs about life that they reinforce. Choose a Tarot deck containing symbolism that holds meaning for you. No matter how valid the philosophy, Astrological symbols won't be helpful to you unless you've studied Astrology. Choose a deck that is full of symbols that intrigue you.

On a less philosophical level, choose a deck that looks good to you. Look for a deck that is attractive in its design. Find one that appeals to your sense of taste and esthetics.

On a more instinctive level, choose a deck that intuitively "feels" right to you. Look at several decks; then sense which one you keep coming back to. Notice which one you think of when you wake up in the morning. Be aware of the deck that captures your fancy for no "logical" reason.

To be practical, choose a deck that is a size and shape that you can easily handle. Your hands will begin to stretch as you shuffle the cards, just as a piano player's hands stretch. But there is no sense in beginning with a deck that is so large or small that it is uncomfortable for you to use.

Finally, feel free to use more than one deck. You may find that several decks appeal to you. You may want to use a given deck for certain moods and another deck for other moods. After tuning in to your own value system, your philosophy, your taste, your intuition, and your hands, choose the decks that "fit" you.

2

THE STRUCTURE
OF A TAROT DECK

A Tarot deck consists of seventy-eight cards—each one uniquely designed. These cards are usually divided into two unequal parts, two sets of 'mysteries' or 'secrets' called arcana. Occasionally, a deck will be numbered and/or organized as one group of seventy-eight cards but in most cases the two-part division is observed. The traditional interpretation of the two parts is that the twenty-two cards of the Major Arcana represent the mysteries or secrets of the universe that are most difficult and important to understand. They will usually be labeled with titles such as The Empress, The Moon or The Lovers. The fifty-six Minor Arcana cards show the simpler, more accessible secrets. They will be designated by number/suit identifications such as The Six of Swords or The Queen of Cups.

When looking at seventy-eight cards, even if they have been divided into two groups, most of us need some way of organizing them so that they are easy to understand as a system. Most people who have studied the Tarot have been faced with the same need. Therefore, numerous systems for categorizing the cards, within each arcana, have been uncovered and created.

THE MAJOR ARCANA SYSTEMS

The twenty-two Major Arcana cards, usually numbered from zero through twenty-one, have been grouped in a variety of ways. In a desire to explain the system of the Major cards, some authors focus on the order of the cards. They see the development of an individual's life depicted in the progression of images from card 0 through card XXI. Many interpreters have applied psychological or spiritual growth theories to this developmental process. For example, the twenty-two Major Arcana cards are often equated with the twenty-two letters of the Hebrew alphabet. These letters correspond with the steps followed in the study of the Kabbalah—the twenty-two steps of the spiritual path from the material world (separation from 'God') back to oneness with 'God.' Some authors move specific cards to new positions to align with their own philosophical interpretations of the growth process. For example, in a move away from the older systems, Waite (designer of the Rider deck which was first published in 1910) placed card 0 between cards XX and XXI and interchanged cards VIII and XI.

Other people are not as concerned with the overall order of the cards as with grouping them within that order. The Major Arcana cards have been analyzed as two groups of eleven cards, three groups of seven cards (plus the 0 card), seven groups of three cards (plus the 0 card), and so forth. Papus, author of *THE TAROT OF THE BOHEMIANS*, addresses the issue of how the cards can be organized in a particularly thorough manner. Each order and system makes sense, in the context of the philosophical system that supports it.

Sally Gearhart, in *A FEMINIST TAROT*, says that the various systems of organizing the Major Arcana cards developed as people created stories or mythologies that would help them remember the attributes of each card. She comments that, by remembering the cards in relationship to each other, we can more easily remember what the individual cards mean.

I worked with a number of mythologies that described the Major Arcana as a system, and became dissatisfied with each one in turn. I have come to the realization that, for me, the greater mysteries of the universe go beyond any one mythology or ordering system. Many of the stories are effective as triggers that can help us remember what the cards mean but too often we get caught up in the limitations of those stories and forget that the myth was just created to help us with our memories. We begin to see the myth as the only truth.

I feel that each Major Arcana card represents a unique, individual concept. I view the concepts as opportunities for growth and expanded awareness, learnings for this world and reality, themes, messages, or basic universal issues. The great concepts stand alone; each one is a learning that we encounter in our lives. No one system describes clearly why or when we meet these issues — the order is different for each individual person. We can sense the patterns, rhythms and cycles that can be shown by grouping the twenty-two Major Arcana cards in various ways. We know that each person unfolds according to her own inner clock, interacting with the cycles in her own way, order and time. The Major Arcana cards show us the universal concepts that we are exploring in our lives; our personal life cycles show us the patterns and sequences in which we develop those concepts. Using our imaginations, we can create personal stories or myths to help us remember the cards' meanings.

The pictorial images on each Major Arcana card represent each artist's opinion of how to best depict the Universal theme, often shown within the context of the author's mythology or philosophical system. Over time, some standardization of these images has occurred. In Chapter 6, I will describe some of the more common images that appear for each Major Arcana card.

THE MINOR ARCANA SYSTEMS

The fifty-six Minor Arcana cards are always divided into four groups or suits. The suits, of fourteen cards each, roughly correspond to the suits of a regular playing card deck. Like a playing card deck, there are numbered cards from Ace through Ten, called pip cards. However, instead of the three face cards of the playing card suits, there are four court cards in each Tarot suit: Page, Knight, Queen and King. (Whether the playing card deck or the Tarot suits came first, historically speaking, or whether they both sprang from another source is a question that hasn't been resolved.)

While many stories have been created to describe the patterns of the Major Arcana, few authors have looked at the development of the Minor Arcana. I feel that it is in the Minor Arcana that we can see the ongoing processes through which we grow and develop. In fact, the fifty-six Minor Arcana cards show us how, within our reality, we experience the universal concepts of the Major Arcana. Each suit represents one method or style through which any Major concept can be experienced. For example, someone might be dealing with boundaries and limits in her life, an issue related to The Devil (a Major card). If The Devil appeared with several cards from the Minor suit of Cups, we could guess that the limits were being experienced in the context of a relationships. Within each suit's realm of activity, we experience growth, in this world, as represented by the numbers from Ace through King.

The four suits, styles, or ways through which we experience the Universal truths are:

SELF AND IDENTITY
UNCONSCIOUS AWARENESS, EMOTION, RELATEDNESS
CONSCIOUS AWARENESS, COMMUNICATION, BELIEFS
PHYSICAL WORLD, SECURITY, GROUNDEDNESS

A variety of symbols can be used to show the development of each of these modes of experience. Some possible symbols for each suit follow:

The Self In This Reality

amoeba reaching   sprout ready   tree, rooted
for experience   to grow   and growing

21

The Emotional/Unconscious World

water   heart   moon

The Mental/Conscious World

lightning   head   sun

The Physical World

money   stone   home

Traditionally, the four Minor Arcana suits of the Tarot are represented by the following names and symbols:

WANDS: Self

CUPS: Unconscious, Emotional World

SWORDS: Conscious, Mental World

PENTACLES: Physical, Material World

Some authors reverse the association of Wands and Swords, applying the growth of self to Swords and mental activity to Wands. I prefer the association I have given and follow that system in this book. There is a thorough discussion of the attributes of each suit in Chapter 4.

ORIENTATION: UPRIGHT OR REVERSED

After you have used your deck for awhile and the cards have become thoroughly mixed, you will notice that some of the cards have turned upside down. An upright card is one that looks right side up while a card that looks upside down is reversed. In doing readings, it's generally desirable that the cards get mixed in this way, so don't worry about trying to keep all the cards facing the same direction.

Cards that have pictures on them clearly have a top and a bottom; it's very easy to tell whether they are upright or reversed after they are laid out on a table. Cards that simply show three cups or seven swords may be harder to figure out. Often a clue is given by the position of the numeral. Other times, you need to be attentive to the orientation of plants, open flowers, and other design elements.

When you and your readee (person getting the reading) are facing each other across a table and the cards are laid out on the table between you, the orientation of the cards is not the same for both of you. To avoid this problem, I usually have the readee sitting next to me, so the cards are facing both of us. On the occasions where the readee is opposite me, I read the cards as facing me. It's up to you to decide which way you want to read them but be consistent once you've decided. That way you'll always know whether a card is reversed or upright in orientation.

In many Tarot texts, different interpretations are given for reversed and upright cards. Often, the reversed card is shown to have the opposite meaning from the upright card. In some books, the authors interpret the cards the same whether they are upright or reversed.

In my work, I have found that the card's orientation does make a difference; however, I don't feel that it makes the radical difference that opposite meanings would indicate. I feel that the basic meaning of the card does not change when it's reversed, but the way the person is experiencing the concept may change quite a bit.

In general, upright cards show that the concept being represented is being experienced by the readee in an obvious, clear, public, or objective way. They show that the person is consciously aware of the issue at hand, may have discussed it with others, and is probably dealing with it or expressing it in an overt manner. The upright card often refers to an event such as buying a house, entering a relationship, or changing how you look. It usually indicates that the energy of the card is being manifested on a "real world" level.

Reversed cards, on the whole, show that the concept is being experienced in a more subtle, private, or secret way. The readee is probably experiencing the issue in a subjective or internalized manner, figuring things out on the inside before they manifest on the outside. The reversal indicates that the card should be interpreted on a more private or personal level. The person may not even be consciously aware of what's going on. But, more often, she's aware of the internal processes that are occurring—it's just that she hasn't publicized them yet.

When this analysis of uprights and reversals is applied to the Major Arcana, interpretations of the cards alter subtly and deepen significantly according to their orientation. You will find each Major card described, in its upright and reversed orientations, in Chapter 6.

In the Minor Arcana, reversals open up possibilities that almost describe four new suits. I say almost because the root concepts of each suit hold true regardless of orientation. Orientation can, however, indicate the emphasis to use in interpreting the cards. That emphasis, within the Minor Arcana, is described below:

General Wands: issues related to self or identity
Upright Wands: the self the public sees
Reversed Wands: private self-image

General Cups:	the emotional or unconscious world
Upright Cups:	relationships; publicly expressed emotions; publicly used psychic skills
Reversed Cups:	intuition; hidden feelings or relationships; relationships to inner parts of self; psychic talents
General Swords:	the mental or conscious world
Upright Swords:	communication; values that are openly manifested through lifestyle
Reversed Swords:	personal beliefs, attitudes or opinions; internal communication
General Pentacles:	the material or physical world
Upright Pentacles:	tangible, physical security; possessions or material goods
Reversed Pentacles:	inner sensation of being safe or grounded in physical reality

As you can tell, the general meaning of the suit applies to both the upright and reversed interpretations but the card's orientation can indicate what's relevant to the current reading. In Chapters 4 and 5, you will find the upright and reversed interpretations of the suits described in greater detail.

In a question of timing, the reversal usually indicates a longer time, a greater delay, or more confusion around the appropriate timing. Chapter 9 goes into this in greater depth.

In general, the experience of the reversed card is more personal, hidden, internal, or subjective. It can sometimes be more ambiguous or vague. It usually shows that the experience of the readee is a private one.

VALUE: NEUTRAL, POSITIVE, OR NEGATIVE

I feel that every Tarot card is basically neutral in value: no card is good or bad in and of itself. However, the energy of each card can be used in helpful and hurtful ways. One easy way to understand this is to look at the influence of rain within our lives. As a natural resource, rain is neutral. It's something we need to survive but it's not good or bad unless we get too much or too little of it. Too much rain can lead to floods while too little rain can result in drought. Depending on the time of year and our location and circumstances, we may see rain as a positive or negative resource in our lives. Similarly, each Tarot card is neutral in essence. And each card can be experienced or used positively or negatively.

When you interpret any card, you can begin by focusing on its essential, neutral meaning. This will describe a concept or process that may be positive or negative for your readee according to her values, growth patterns, previous experiences, and current situation. For example, one readee might be experiencing the boundaries of The Devil as traps, cages, and uncomfortable limits. To another person, the boundaries represent structure, definition, and a sense of direction. Remember, too, that what's positive for you may be a problem for your readee; what you feel is a struggle may be a breeze for her. Based on her feedback, the question being asked, and your intuition, you can stretch the neutral interpretation of a card into its positive or negative application.

As you work with the interpretations in this book, you'll find that I've given neutral as well as positive and negative applications for all the cards. In Chapter 8, there is more information on how to apply value to a card according to its layout position.

*   *   *   *   *

Now, you have a general picture of the Tarot. As you can see, the organization of the deck is closely related to the interpretation of the cards. Each author will therefore organize (and interpret) the cards according to her own philosophy of life. As you explore the Tarot, you will find more and more associations between your understanding of the world and the cards. As you become aware of strong correlations, apply them to your interpretations, test them, see if they hold true for you. I know of some readers who have strong individual systems of ordering the cards that are exactly perfect for them and exactly ineffective for anyone else. Use my system of analysis only as your beginning point in discovering the many patterns that the Tarot describes.

3

THE DEVELOPMENT
OF NUMBER

In Chapter 2, I explained that the Tarot is divided into two groups called arcana and that the Minor Arcana is further divided into four suits, which are numbered from Ace through King. Now, I'll continue with a more thorough explanation of the cards by looking at the Minor Arcana and its numerical development.

The symbols for number seem to be the least confusing and limiting of all the symbols. They allow us to get at basic concepts, somewhat free of our own attitudes and the attitudes of those who have designed the cards. Number symbols allow us to start with something very familiar to us — a pile of stones or the numeral 7 — and progress from there.

Most people, in our culture, are familiar with the Arabic Numerals (1, 2, 3, 4), some are familiar with Roman Numerals (I, II, III, IV), and all of us are familiar with groups of objects. When we explore the meaning of number concepts, we are exploring the meaning of the number, the meaning of "six-ness: the quality of being six," not the numeral 6 or the picture of six wands. The pictures and the numerals are simply symbols that help us understand the quality and basic meaning of the number.

When we deal with the number concepts of one through nine, we are dealing with core concepts: all other numbers can be reduced to these concepts. The reduction process is not any of the "methods" that we learn in school but it is amazingly similar to the approach that many children take when they are first learning to add numbers of more than one digit. In the study of the Tarot no reducing needs to be done, but I've included some examples of the reduction process here for your information:

$$461 = 4+6+1 = 11 = 1+1 = 2$$
$$7293 = 7+2+9+3 = 21 = 2+1 = 3$$
$$26 = 2+6 = 8$$

Any number can eventually be reduced to one of the numbers from one through nine. Ten, One Hundred, One Thousand, and so forth are special numbers because they go directly back to one, the beginning. They can be seen as numbers that allow for transitions to new beginnings:

$$10 = 1+0 = 1$$
$$10,000 = 1+0+0+0+0 = 1$$

By assigning numerical values to letters of the alphabet, to events, to feelings, or to issues, complex situations can be broken down to the interaction of nine basic energies, plus the energy of transition. Within the nine energies, each number concept builds on the concept of the number that comes before it and leads to the one that comes after it. The meanings develop as follows:

THIS: Something new is established.

THAT: Something challenges, confronts, changes, or expands THIS.

THE   The interaction between THIS and THAT is resolved and
OTHER: integrated by an encompassing whole.

THIS: Another new thing is established, building on THE OTHER, etc.

The number concepts develop in groups of three: each group shows a new way in which the interaction or contrast between THIS and THAT can be resolved. After three groups of three (a giant set of THIS, THAT, and THE OTHER), after the point of nine-ness, the opportunity for transition occurs: the ten.

In my own work with the Tarot, understanding the concepts of THIS, THAT, and THE OTHER opened up a whole new way of thinking. I was able to take concepts that seemed polarized, THIS and THAT, and find ways of unifying them into wholes: THE OTHER. I'll share some of my insights with you.

Most of us tend to feel that our lives are divided into categories. We especially like the two-part divisions of dichotomies like these:

win-lose	wrong-right
male-female	yin-yang
inside-outside	conscious-subconscious
above-below	bad-good
body-spirit	positive-negative
work-play	forward-backward
earth-sky	past-future
active-passive	dark-light

NONE OF THESE POLARITIES ARE AS IMPORTANT AS THE WHOLES THAT UNITE THEM.

The important part of the yin/yang symbol is not the black or the white part or the way they balance or contrast with each other. The important part is the circle that unites them. For every polarity, there is a whole that unites the parts.

FOR EXAMPLE:

I have finally realized that I am a whole person, not a half-person expecting another to make me whole. I can unify qualities of

29

"femininity" and "masculinity" within myself. I am the whole that unifies those qualities.

My body and spirit form a whole. I've spent a lot of time fighting my body and affirming my spirit but neither works well without the other. I needed to see that I am the whole that unites my body and spirit.

My unconscious or intuitive awareness is not separate from my conscious mind. Both are valuable parts of my total awareness.

I don't need to characterize my feelings as "good" or "bad." All of them are valid and useful. All of them help me to understand my self and the ways I experience life.

The past and the future are not fixed things: they are really only probabilities based on our linear notion of time. From the present, we can certainly choose to experience the past differently, to remember different parts with more or less intensity. By our selective experience of the past, we actually change the reality of that past. And, we always have the option of creating the future that we want by changing our actions in the present. The present is the whole that contains our past and our future.

No life is complete without work; no life is complete without play. Both play and work need to be satisfying and meaningful; together they create a productive balance.

If I'm right, you can be right, too. If I win, you can win, too. My needs do not have to be met at your expense. There is a way that both of us can be satisfied. There is always THE OTHER way that encompasses both of our needs.

These are a few of the insights that I've gained over the years through my work with the Tarot as well as my study of other philosophies. The core idea, the "cycle of three" is embodied beautifully in the Tarot. We can apply that idea to many areas of our lives, to all the issues that seem so divided and polarized.

The cycle of three is primarily applicable to the Minor Arcana, the part of the Tarot that develops linearly. Within the fourteen cards of each suit, there are four cycles of three, one point of transition, and one point of completion. Each of the cycles and each of the other points has its own character and nature. The following discussion of the development of number is applicable to each of the four suits. Within each suit, the basic concepts are interpreted according to the focus of that suit. Specific applications to each suit are in Chapter 4.

THE MEANING OF NUMBER IN THE MINOR ARCANA

1 2 3

First Cycle Of Three: The Conceptual Level
Something is conceived and articulated.

ONE-NESS (ACE): A POINT

This is the beginning. Something new exists at this point. A seed has been planted, something has been conceived. Something has begun but you don't yet know where it will lead or how it will be defined or developed. You're not even sure it will lead anywhere. It may be only the possibility of a new direction; the seed may sit in the ground and never grow. However, the Aces embody potential growth in new directions. They symbolize the urge to initiate new things.

TWO-NESS: A LINE

A second point comes onto the scene here. The purpose of the Two is to solidify or confirm the direction of the Ace. At the level of the Two, you are watering and fertilizing a seed, claiming, naming, or affirming something that has already been initiated. You are saying a more definite "yes" to something that was barely a possibility at the Ace level. In order to clearly confirm the direction, you may need to compare the option with something else. In that case you can only choose and give energy to one seed after you have contrasted it with other seeds that have been sown. You may appear to be blocking the progress of the One as you weigh and balance it against other options. However, the ultimate aim of the Two is to choose, affirm, stabilize, or claim the One's direction.

THREE-NESS: A PLANE

Now you have the unification of the aggressive energy of the One with the stabilizing energy of the Two. A third point allows you to get some distance and perspective on the first two. It allows you to observe the first two points and become aware of the full potential of their interaction. You can see, in detail, how One and Two join forces to evolve and grow. You recognize that what seemed to be blocking the One's expansion was only a process of deliberation. At the level of the Three, you can clearly see the whole picture. You can see that both the aggressive and stabilizing energies are needed in order for your new direction or idea to be actualized. The Three level is the level of clarification, refinement, and articulation. It is the level of planning. Here, you take many details into account and thoroughly prepare to put your plan into action.

4 5 6

Second Cycle of Three: The Actualized Level
Something is manifested and adusted.

FOUR-NESS: A SOLID

Up to now, your new direction has existed only on the "ideal" plane, in two dimensions. At the point of the Four, you are ready to make something that has only been a plan or a blueprint into something that is three dimensional. The Four is the level of creating something in time and space. There is a solid sense about the Four, a feeling that something has finally been actualized. There is also a tendency to see it as an unchanging, firmly established, permanent entity. As a result, the Four is sometimes experienced as stubbornness and determination to hang on to what's been created.

FIVE-NESS: TIME

The thing that seemed so solid at the Four level is now being challenged. Through the process of time, even solid matter changes and moves. The thing that seemed so well-established at the Four is meeting a reaction, receiving feedback, being affected. It is being forced to adapt, change, or shift ground. Sometimes it seems like everything's in upheaval and confusion at the Five level. You may also experience the Five in a more subtle way as a feeling of shifting sands, disquiet, discomfort, and uneasiness. Things are not as secure or solid as they seemed at the Four. The Five is encouraging you to adjust, adapt, or change your original plan as a result of testing it in the real world. Depending on your resistance to the change, you can experience the five as a gentle nudge or as a large club hitting you on the head.

SIX-NESS: CYCLE

Now you've seen that your creations are affected by time and you realize that everything adapts and changes through time. At the Six level, you create a rhythm or cycle that allows you to feel solid and yet ride comfortably with the waves. It is a simple, repetitive cycle or pattern that seems harmonious and peaceful. There is a feeling of getting centered after upheaval, of reaching a plateau or resting place, a calmness AFTER the storm. You have created a pattern that will stand the test of time and hold up under most circumstances. The pattern of activity or behavior is comfortable and it's predictable.

7 8 9

Third Cycle Of Three: The Expanded Level
Something is developed, explored, and expanded.

SEVEN-NESS: IMAGINATION

The repeated rhythm and harmony of the Six has become a bit repetitious and even boring. Now it's time to experiment and get some variety into things. Here, you are adding new variations to the melody you've created. You are very busy, dabbling in many areas, expanding your awareness and activities. You are playing with various possibilities without committing to any of them. The Seven is the level of variety, expansion, experimentation, and imagination. You've had enough experience now, in Ace through Six, to know how and where you might stretch and vary things to allow for a broader experience.

EIGHT-NESS: ORDER

All the activity of the Seven is eventually somewhat tiring; the level of Eight is a reaction to that fatigue. It's time to re-evaluate and prioritize what's been happening at the Seven level. If Sevens are expansion, Eights are contraction. You stop and think about all the possibilities and experiences and begin to sort out those you want to keep from those you want to discard. It's a time of thought, reorganization, and ordering; a time of putting things in their places according to their relative values. The Eight level is one of establishing priorities and getting organized.

NINE-NESS: INTEGRATION

Now that you've got your priorities established, you are ready to integrate all your activities into a flexible pattern of forward motion. You are not simply establishing a sense of center after confusion as you were at the Six level; you are not merely creating a repetitive, cyclical pattern. You are taking your own priorities and values into account, after much experience, and reaching a place of clear integration and ongoing direction. There is a sense of flow among the parts of yourself or between you and the world. You feel you are in the process of living, being, and moving. At the Nine level, you combine the expansion and imagination of the Seven with the contraction and order of the Eight: the result is integrated forward motion.

10

Transition Point
Something has been successfully developed.
You have a choice about what to do with it.

TEN-NESS: TRANSITION

You have been working with the system that you integrated at the Nine level for a while now. It is working well but you know that you need to challenge yourself or you will stagnate in the ease and familiarity of it. You are aware that you can choose to re-commit to the already established direction and get deeper into it—or you can begin something new. Both of those options involve some unknowns and so you feel hesitant about making the choice. You know you can't stay here, on the brink of transition, forever. You are aware that your choice involves the risk of losing what you already have for the sake of something better. For now, it's easier, and even appropriate, to hesitate, to hold back, to sit on the fence for a moment, enjoy the respite, and postpone the decision.

The remaining four levels are represented by the unnumbered Court cards: Page, Knight, Queen, and King. They form a cycle of three and complete the suits.

P K Q

Fourth Cycle Of Three: The Fulfilled Level
Something reaches its full potential and maturity.

PAGE-NESS: RISK

You've decided to re-commit to a direction that's already been established. You know that it can't just be the old way and that you will have to challenge yourself and take some risks to take it into a new level of meaning. You are afraid of being disappointed. You are aware that you need to be courageous in order to take this step because you could lose everything you have if the risk doesn't pay off. However, you have calculated the odds and you have hopes that the situation will become more satisfying if you make a renewed commitment. The Page is the level of risk-taking, of daring to re-commit to something that is not a sure bet. You are re-committing in order to take something from the Nine level of integration to an even higher level of excellence and maturity.

KNIGHT-NESS: FOCUS

Now that you've committed yourself, you're totally involved. At the level of the Knight, you are completely immersed in your activity or direction. Everything else seems irrelevant. There is a sense of complete focus, absolute dedication, and intensity. Your energy is fully directed toward the accomplishment of your goal and the deepening of your commitment. Since you've taken such a big risk at the Page level, all your Knight energy is focused on making the risk pay off. Nothing else matters for now.

QUEEN-NESS: MATURITY

All of the focus and work of the Knight is finally reaching fulfillment. You have deep and thoroughly developed skills, along with the confidence that comes from wisdom and vast experience. You know when to adapt and when to stand firm. You don't really need to learn anything new about this thing. You are already capable of working with it as you continue to grow and evolve. This direction or project is satisfying to you because it is flexible and changeable, yet familiar and manageable. You have a depth of understanding about this thing that is unique and valuable. With the Queen, you are at the level of deepest maturity and competence.

Completion Point
You have completed a cycle that began at the Ace.
You are ready to let go of the past
and begin a new cycle.

KING-NESS: COMPLETION

You've gotten as much as you can out of this cycle, activity, or process. There really is nothing left to gain by remaining in this space. All that's left is the brittle shell or husk of what used to be. It is clear that the old situation is drained dry for you, used up, ended. It's time to move on, transform yourself, and establish a new direction. You know that you are done with it but you also sense a need to symbolize the completion through some kind of ritual or gesture. After the completion, you will be able to move on and begin a new cycle. The King is the level of letting go, releasing, and completing old things. The important thing to remember at the King level is to have respect for the past. With all due appreciation for what has gone before, you're now ready to move on.

4

THE FOUR SUITS

Each of the four suits of the Minor Arcana develops in the manner I've described in Chapter 3. Because each suit governs or represents its own area of life, the basic concepts of the numbers are adapted and applied to each of those areas. Applications to the suits are included in Chapter 5. However, once you thoroughly understand the number concepts and the suit concepts, you can actually combine the meanings and create the interpretations for yourself.

As you work with the Minor Arcana, remember to maintain as much flexibility as you can. Each suit represents a broad range of issues. You will need to use your own intuition as well as feedback from your readee to insure that you are focusing on the appropriate issue.

The linear order of the suit cards is a system that helps us understand a whole life process. In our own lives, we may not follow that exact order; however we can understand a given stage in development by looking at the number levels that come before and after it. We can give our readees a sense of what has led to the current situation and a feeling of how it could grow and develop.

Each of us is growing in all the areas represented by the four suits. Even within each area, we may be simultaneously at a Three level, an Eight level, and a Queen level. We may jump from the Eight to the Five when a new curve is thrown our way. We may leap from a

Seven to a Knight when we discover something that really commands our attention. The purpose of this system is to lend some order to our awareness. Once we understand the system, we need to be flexible with it.

As you explore the suits and create correspondences between them and the numbers, feel free to adapt the meanings of the cards as you see fit. Once you have made a change in interpretation, stick to it for awhile, test it, see if it really works in your readings. As long as you are clear on what each card means for you, the Universe will use your language and the appropriate cards will turn up.

On the following pages are descriptions of the suits. I would like to note that my compass directions are taken from Astrological correspondences between the elements and the directions. Those who study and practice Witchcraft as a religion or philosophy may use a different set of compass directions for the elements:

WITCHCRAFT   ASTROLOGY

Fire: South   Water: West   Fire: East   Water: North
Air: East   Earth: North   Air: West   Earth: South

THE SUIT OF WANDS

NUMBER OF THE SUIT: one
OTHER NAMES FOR THE SUIT: Batons, Staves, Rods
CORRESPONDING PLAYING CARD SUIT: Clubs
ELEMENT: Fire
SEASON: Spring
DIRECTIONS: East, Left, Forward
BASIC NATURE: progressing, acting, future-oriented

Basic Interpretation: Wands represent the growth and awareness of the SELF and all its potential. The identity and the ego are involved in the process of truly naming the self. With Wands, you are concerned with discovering your true self, apart from others. You are exploring who you are, alone, individually. You are discovering and uncovering pride in yourself and your creativity. You are sensing your own personal direction. You are naming the roles you want to play and the hats you want to wear. You are asking, "Who am I and where am I going?" and "How can I creatively express who I am?"

Upright Wands refer to the self you're presenting to the world, the public self, the role everyone sees you playing, the way others view you.

Reversed Wands refer to your self-image, the way you view who you are, your self-concept, and the self you are in your private life.

THE SUIT OF CUPS

NUMBER OF THE SUIT: two
OTHER NAMES FOR THE SUIT: Coupes
CORRESPONDING PLAYING CARD SUIT: Hearts
ELEMENT: Water
SEASON: Summer
DIRECTIONS: North, Right, Backward
BASIC NATURE: centering, securing what exists;
                     building on past foundations

Basic Interpretation: Cups represent the growth and awareness of the UNCONSCIOUS and the feelings that arise from it. Cups represent your emotional interactions and relationships with others. Since your unconscious is also the gateway to spiritual awareness and psychic activity, you can become aware, through the Suit of Cups, of being a part of the whole Universe. You are asking "What are my emotional needs and how do I meet them?" and "How am I connected to the Universe on an unconscious level?"

Upright Cups refer to the emotions and feelings that you share and openly express. They refer to relationships that are publicly acknowledged. Occasionally, an upright Cups card will refer to psychic or spiritual activity that occurs in a public sphere.

Reversed Cups can refer to private, or hidden emotions or relationships. They can indicate the relationship between internal parts of yourself. Usually, reversed Cups refer to the development of psychic and intuitive abilities. They describe the deeply personal ways in which we experience our unconscious awareness.

THE SUIT OF SWORDS

NUMBER OF THE SUIT: three
OTHER NAMES FOR THE SUIT: Epees
CORRESPONDING PLAYING CARD SUIT: Spades
ELEMENT: Air
SEASON: Fall
DIRECTIONS: West, Left, Up
BASIC NATURE: progressing, acting, future-oriented

Basic Interpretation: Swords represent the growth and development of the CONSCIOUS MIND. Here, you are developing your thoughts and ideas as well as your system of beliefs. You are acting on your philosophy of life. The Swords also reflect the connectedness between ideas. You are involved in the processes of communication and discussion. You are asking "What do I think and how do I share, teach or act out what I think?" and "What is my philosophy of life and how does my lifestyle reflect that philosophy?"

Upright Swords refer to the lifestyle that you visibly act out for others to see. They show the ways in which you manifest your philosophy in obvious, public forms. Upright Swords reflect your communication processes as well as the schedules and day-to-day routines by which you live.

Reversed Swords refer to the beliefs and attitudes that are behind your day-to-day lifestyle. These personal philosophical ideas and ideals lie beneath the opinions you publicly express. Reversed Swords can also refer to secret communication or communication between inner parts of yourself.

THE SUIT OF PENTACLES

NUMBER OF THE SUIT: four
OTHER NAMES FOR THE SUIT: Disks, Deniers, Coins
CORRESPONDING PLAYING CARD SUIT: Diamonds
ELEMENT: Earth
SEASON: Winter
DIRECTIONS: South, Right, Down
BASIC NATURE: Centering, securing what exists;
                building on past foundations

Basic Interpretation: Pentacles represent the growth and development of GROUNDEDNESS in the material, physical world. With Pentacles, you are concerned with your financial security, home, car, and other material resources. You are concerned with your job, career, or work in the world. You are dealing with your body, health, and physical or sexual activities. With Pentacles, you are asking "What are my physical and security needs and how do I meet them?" and "How am I grounded in the material world?"

Upright Pentacles refer to the obvious, outward manifestations of your security. They reflect circumstances surrounding your house, job, car, money, and so on. They show you what's going on with your health or sexual activities.

Reversed Pentacles refer to a subtler sense of being grounded, centered, and secure within the world. They will show how safe you feel interacting with physical/material things, how comfortable you feel with being alive in a physical body. They also describe your level of connectedness with the Earth. They may, occasionally, indicate a hidden health condition.

5

THE MINOR ARCANA

In this chapter, you'll find interpretations of the Minor Arcana cards. They are organized by number so that you can easily see the correspondences between all the Twos, Eights, and so forth. The neutral, positive and negative meanings for each number are discussed and the upright and reversed interpretations for each card are described.

As you work with these interpretations, be conscious of the overall area of life that is ruled by each suit and the concept that is embodied in each number. One or more of the given interpretations may fit your readee's situation. You will not find descriptions of all the possible applications of each suit/number combination. Your intuition and your readee's feedback will tell you how to combine the suit and number concepts in the interpretation of any particular card.

THE ACES: BEGINNING

The images on the Aces show the potential for new beginnings. Many decks show the suit symbols being held out in space, existing as a potential, not yet attached or anchored in the real world. In other decks, the Aces may include symbols of birth, seeds or young babies.

Neutral: All the Aces initiate new beginnings. They show that something fresh is starting. The seed for a whole new form is being planted.

Positive: It's a good time to plant the seeds for something new because the seed will grow into something that will be of benefit to you.

Negative: You're probably jumping the gun. You may have some old business to complete before you rush into new projects. Or, given the circumstances, a fresh start will be ineffective.

ACE OF WANDS: A New Identity

Upright: You are planting the seeds for a new, public identity. You're beginning to create a new name for yourself or take on a new role in life.

Reversed: You sense the potential for creating a new self-image or self-concept. You can privately name yourself in a new way.

45

ACE OF CUPS: A New Emotion or Insight

Upright: You're feeling something new, maybe something you haven't felt before. It might be a new emotion, a new relationship, or a new awareness about an existing relationship. The seed of love, anger, jealousy or another emotion has been planted.

Reversed: The potential for new intuitive or psychic experiences now exists. You are setting things in motion that could open up your psychic potential. You may even be having psychic flashes. This could also represent the beginning of a secret relationship or hidden feelings.

ACE OF SWORDS: A New Idea

Upright: You are aware of the potential for a brand new lifestyle direction or schedule. You recognize that you could begin to communicate in a different way. There is the possibility for you to manifest your philosophy in a new way.

Reversed: You are aware that you could create new beliefs, attitudes and opinions within yourself. In fact, you might already have planted the seeds for the creation of these new beliefs. A different world-view or philosophy is possible.

ACE OF PENTACLES: A New Physical Form or Pattern

Upright: You are planting seeds for a new home, job, career, or form of security. You may be getting a new sense of how to work with money and finances. You may be getting some urges to begin a new physical regime or a new direction in your health.

Reversed: You can potentially create a new form or level of safety and stability in your life. You could experience a new kind of groundedness or centeredness. You may feel the stirrings of a new connection with natural, earthy forces.

2

THE TWOS: AFFIRMING

The images of the Two cards usually show two cups, two swords, etc. In most decks there is a sense of affirmation about the picture or at least a sense that some choice, pledge, or commitment is being made. Sometimes, the picture shows someone balancing two options in the very act of deciding which one to confirm.

Neutral: The Twos represent the affirmation and confirmation of new directions that were begun at the Ace level. You're comparing your options and choosing to say "yes" to the Ace's beginning but you haven't yet fully developed the plan of the Three.

Positive: It's appropriate to say "yes" to this new thing. It's to your advantage to claim it for your own. Even though the details aren't clear yet, this is an appropriate direction for you.

Negative: Choosing and affirming isn't appropriate right now. You could be choosing something that isn't good for you or you may not have enough data to make a choice at this time. It's also possible that you've already made the choice and it's time to move on to planning (Three). In any case, it's inappropriate to focus on choosing now.

TWO OF WANDS: Claiming and Validating the Self

Upright: You are validating yourself. You are saying "yes" to a new role that you've definitely decided to play. You may have decided to pursue this identity as a result of comparing and contrasting it with other possibilities. At this point you are naming the new identity and claiming it for your own.

Reversed: You are affirming or claiming a new self-concept. Though others may not be aware of it, you have personally named and accepted a part of yourself that you may have previously ignored.

TWO OF CUPS: Validating a Feeling

Upright: You are choosing or naming a feeling or relationship. You are accepting and validating what you feel. You may be publicly or consciously claiming, naming, or nurturing an emotional or sensitive part of yourself.

Reversed: You are validating or claiming a psychic or intuitive experience. You are choosing to open up to that inner part of yourself and accept your own psychic talents. You could also be connecting with some private feelings or choosing a secret relationship.

TWO OF SWORDS: Affirming a Philosophy or Lifestyle

Upright: You are saying "yes" to using a new type of communication or language. You are consciously or publicly confirming a new lifestyle or schedule. You've decided that you want to "speak up" about something though you haven't planned what to say yet. You are nurturing an idea.

Reversed: You are identifying and affirming a new belief, attitude, or opinion. You are claiming it as "true" for you. You are identifying, naming and choosing affirmations for your life.

TWO OF PENTACLES: Choosing a Physical Path

Upright: You are affirming and nurturing a new form of financial or material security. You may be conserving and maintaining physical resources or your own physical energy. You are saying "yes" to a new direction for home, career, money, resources, or your physical body.

Reversed: You are recognizing and affirming the need for a new security base. You are nurturing and confirming a particular direction that would help to establish a different pattern of stability in your life. You are choosing and affirming a new kind of groundedness or inner stability.

3

THE THREES: PLANNING

The pictures on the Threes usually show people who are preparing to take action. They may be looking at a path, seeking advice from an expert, or studying plans. The Threes may also symbolize the unity that is needed between several elements or people before a plan can be put into action.

Neutral: You are planning and preparing yourself. You are putting all the details in place before you begin the actual work. You have chosen your direction (Two) and now you are clarifying things as much as you can, prior to taking action (Four).

Positive: Planning, articulation and clarification are needed now. It's a good idea to get as much clarity, advice, or insight as possible before taking action.

Negative: You're spending too much time refining your plans. You might need to go ahead and put your plans into action. You could also be trying to clarify something that you haven't named or claimed (Two) yet. For now, planning is inappropriate.

THREE OF WANDS: Defining and Clarifying the Identity

Upright: You are beginning to really understand and see yourself more clearly. You are defining the new roles you want to play and making plans for presenting your new self to the world.

49

Reversed: You are seeing yourself in a detailed and complete manner. You are clarifying your self-image and sense of personal direction. You are making plans for becoming the self you privately want to be.

THREE OF CUPS: Emotional or Intuitive Clarification

Upright: You are getting much clearer about what you feel. You can name your feelings or understand an emotional pattern that you've been in. You see how your relationship is working. You are clarifying your true feelings. You are planning what you want to do regarding a particular emotion or relationship. You might be getting ready to "go public" with your psychic abilities.

Reversed: You are getting clearer on what your intuition is telling you. You are aware of your dreams, visions, or psychic insights and how they are helpful in your life. You are making plans through an intuitive, not cognitive, process. You might be making plans regarding a secret relationship or emotion.

THREE OF SWORDS: Planning a Philosophy or Lifestyle

Upright: You are clarifying and articulating what you really think, prior to presentation or publication. You are looking at your chosen lifestyle and planning how to implement it into your daily schedule. You are figuring out how to communicate what you want to say.

Reversed: You are clarifying your personal attitudes and opinions. You have chosen your beliefs and now you're beginning to understand them in greater detail. You are planning how you might experience what's "true" for you. You might be getting ready for hidden or secret communication.

THREE OF PENTACLES: Planning Secure Structures

Upright: You are clearly articulating the nature of material and financial security that you want or don't want. You're defining the kinds of physical, financial, career or family stability that you want. You are making plans for creating that physical formation.

Reversed: You are clarifying the kinds of security needs that you really have. You're defining the things that give you that inner sense of safety and groundedness. You're preparing to take action that will make you feel more connected with the earth.

THE FOURS: MANIFESTING

The Fours often show people who are taking steps and actively creating what they've planned. You may also see people hanging on to what they've created in a stubborn or inflexible manner.

Neutral: The Fours show the manifestation of plans into reality. Things that were previously imagined or visualized (Three) have now become real. Now that they are real, it will soon be time to adjust (Five) and improve on the original construction.

Positive: It's appropriate to put your plan into action. Go ahead and create what you've designed. Act out what you think or feel. Do it.

Negative: A Four can be a problem if you haven't done enough planning (Three). You may be trying to manifest something before you're really prepared for it. You could also be holding on too tightly to what you've created. You need to be adapting what you've created (Five).

FOUR OF WANDS: Manifesting a New Identity

Upright: Now that you know who you are and have a sense of direction, you are acting on it. You are taking the concrete, obvious steps toward putting the new you out into the world. You are publicly naming yourself. You are doing something definite about showing who you

51

are; you're making a clear statement about yourself.

Reversed: You are taking action based on your view of yourself. On a personal level, you have clearly defined who you want to be. Now, you're creating that self. No one else may see it but you know you are taking definite steps toward becoming the new you and manifesting your chosen self-image.

FOUR OF CUPS: Acting on What You Feel

Upright: Now that you know what you're feeling, you're acting on it. You're doing something to express your emotions. You may be taking some steps toward creating a relationship or toward showing your emotions.

Reversed: You are acting on your psychic or intuitive perceptions and beginning to make your dreams and visions "come true." You are taking steps regarding your psychic activities. You might also be acting on a hidden emotion or relationship.

FOUR OF SWORDS: Acting on What You Think

Upright: You're acting on your ideas. You're publicly manifesting your philosophy and commmunicating your point of view. You may be explaining an idea, saying what you think, sending a letter, or writing what you've outlined. You could be acting out the lifestyle or schedule that you've envisioned and planned.

Reversed: You're privately manifesting your philosophy. You're taking quiet action based on your attitudes, opinions, and beliefs. You are having internal conversations with parts of yourself. Or, you could be talking about someone behind her back! The communication that's happening is not public.

FOUR OF PENTACLES: Making Something Tangible

Upright: You are taking concrete steps toward creating security in the physical world. You are buying the house, applying for the job, or starting an exercise program. You are publicly taking physical, measurable action toward accomplishing a project in the "real" world.

Reversed: You are privately taking action in order to create the kind of security you want to have. You are doing whatever you need to do to feel safe, secure, and stabilized. You are connecting with the physical earth or taking other action related to feeling grounded and centered.

5

THE FIVES: ADJUSTING

The images of the Fives usually show some kind of change, distress, or challenge. They often reflect the author's feeling that change and adjustment are uncomfortable processes. In some decks you will find the Fives represented by someone who is molding or adapting something that already exists.

Neutral: The Fives demonstrate the need for change and adjustment. They appear when you are getting internal or external feedback about your actions. This information is allowing you to test and adapt whatever you've created (Four) and helping you to work out the "kinks" so that you can move on to the steady reliability of the Six.

Positive: You are successfully adapting as a result of feedback. You have seen the results of your actions and are now making adjustments to your original plan. It's appropriate to change your plans or adapt yourself at this point.

Negative: These changes and adjustments are not appropriate. You need to stop all the shifting around and quit reacting to every bit of feedback. You may be changing too much, too soon. At this point, change could indicate upheaval, discomfort, or even catastrophe.

FIVE OF WANDS: Adjusting the Identity

Upright: You are being challenged to adapt and grow. You are adjusting the way you present yourself to others. You could be experiencing an identity crisis. You might be getting some feedback from the environment that challenges you to reconsider the role you're playing and make some adjustments in it.

Reversed: You are challenging yourself to adapt and change. You are pushing yourself to adjust your self-image until it feels more positive or appropriate. You might be experiencing self doubt. Whatever the world sees, you know you are changing yourself.

FIVE OF CUPS: Emotional or Intuitive Adjustments

Upright: Your feelings are in flux. Everything that seemed emotionally sure, now feels as though it's changing and shifting. You are adapting your emotional foundations. You may be sensing emotional uncertainty, discomfort or confusion. You may be feeling vulnerable. Your feelings and relationships are being challenged. Old feelings or relationships that weren't resolved in the past may be re-emerging for current resolution.

Reversed: You are feeling challenged on a psychic or intuitive plane. You may be experiencing something on the psychic level that is making you feel uneasy. You are making adjustments in the ways you use your intuition. You could also be going through some private emotional adjustments.

FIVE OF SWORDS: Philosophical Adjustments

Upright: Your lifestyle is being challenged or changed. You are aware of the limitations of a given philosophy as you act it out in your daily life. Your communication patterns may be in flux as a result of feedback from others. You could be adjusting (editing) something you've written or said.

54

Reversed: You're getting feedback that's encouraging you (or forcing you) to change your beliefs and attitudes. Opinions and ideas that you thought were "true" are going through a process of adjustment and change. You may even feel confused or unsure about your chosen beliefs. Others may not see it, but you're challenging and changing your attitudes.

FIVE OF PENTACLES: Physical Adjustments

Upright: Your security is being changed or adjusted in some way. You may be feeling confused or doubtful about the value of things that seemed stable to you. Something about your "home" base is shifting. You may be experiencing some changes in your health. There may be some adjustments in your career, job, or financial situation.

Reversed: You're experiencing shifts and adjustments in your inner sense of security or centeredness. You may feel that your basic groundedness is being challenged. You're changing the ways in which you feel connected with the earth. You're altering or questioning your "security blanket."

THE SIXES: CYCLING

The images of the Sixes usually show contentment, relaxation, satisfaction or even victory over the challenges of the Fives. There is often a sense of motion but the motion is not sudden or startling; it's steady and reliable.

Neutral: The Sixes represent the calm AFTER the storm. Life is proceeding in a rhythmic, predictable pattern after the upheaval or adjustment of the Five. The cycles are regular and few surprises are in store. The Sixes show your habitual behavior. They give you the security to expand with the Sevens.

Positive: It's to your advantage to rest, relax, and take things easy for awhile. Since you know what to expect, you don't need to worry or put energy into anticipating what will happen. You can just go with the rhythm.

Negative: You're frustrated and bored by repeating the same cycle over and over again. In this case, knowing what to expect is not to your advantage. The rhythmic, predictable pace is monotonous or downright problematical for you. You could also be trying, inappropriately, to repeat a pattern that still needs more adjustment (Five).

SIX OF WANDS: A Predictable Personality

Upright: You've met the challenge to your identity and come through it. Now, the self you're presenting to the world is more consistent and stable. You feel more secure with your identity and sense of purpose or personal direction. You're settling into the groove of being this self.

Reversed: You've reached a level of stability with your sense of self-worth. You've finished challenging yourself and feel more sure of who you are. You are consistently viewing yourself through a particular self-image. No matter what happens, you see yourself that way.

SIX OF CUPS: A Regular Emotional Cycle

Upright: Your relationship is reaching a level of understanding that is more reliable and predictable. You are feeling more secure about your feelings, knowing that they won't be drastically changing. You know what to expect from yourself and others on an emotional level.

Reversed: Your psychic and intuitive processes are more predictable now. You can count on certain emotional tools to work for you in familiar and recognizable ways. You may be experiencing a consistent pattern in your dreams, visions, or fantasies. You could also be experiencing a reliable, but secret, relationship.

SIX OF SWORDS: A Reliable Philosophy and Lifestyle

Upright: You're reintegrating your daily lifestyle after some challenge and confusion. It now reflects a rhythmic and cyclical pattern. You can rely on certain spoken or written communication patterns—they are predictable and regular.

Reversed: You are repeatedly affirming certain beliefs or attitudes. The more you repeat them, the truer they seem. Your beliefs and attitudes are no longer being challenged or attacked. Now, they are simply accepted and reiterated.

SIX OF PENTACLES: A Predictable Physical Cycle

Upright: Your income or security is steady and predictable. Your money, home or business cycles are more regular and reliable. You have weathered the physical storm and are now experiencing a period of balanced or stabilized health. You are repeating a familiar pattern in the material world. You can mass produce a product because you know you've corrected the errors. You may be replenishing your reserves after a period of using them up.

Reversed: You are re-centering yourself and re-establishing your security base after a period of confusion or challenge. You find that certain patterns tend to create a sense of security or safety for you so you repeat those patterns regularly. You know that you can rely on these patterns to create a predictable and calming sense of peace.

7

THE SEVENS: IMAGINING

The images of the Sevens usually indicate someone who's faced with a variety of options. The person is reaching out to grasp these multiple options, wanting to experience as many of them as possible.

Neutral: With the Sevens, you're stretching out to seek variety and expansion. You are experimenting with some new aspects of something that's been reliably established in the Six. You're playing around with possibilities, stretching the potential of whatever has already been developed.

Positive: This variety is creating an interesting and stimulating life for you. It's not necessary right now to make firm commitments (Eight) it's more appropriate to experiment. Your need is to gather information and experiences so that you will have plenty of data for future decision making.

Negative: You have too much going on. You're overextended, flitting around, or too active. You might need to slow down, make commitments and get organized (Eight) or you might need to go back and establish a more reliable system (Six) before you start experimenting. In any case, the current amount of variety and stimulation is inappropriate for you.

SEVEN OF WANDS: Experimenting with Different Roles

Upright: You were beginning to feel a bit one-dimensional. Now you want to explore some new aspects of yourself. It's time to experiment a little with who you can be, try on some new hats, play around with some new roles that you might adopt. You might explore how you function in a variety of situations or explore the variety of selves that you can be in a single situation. You are discovering the many facets of your personality and expanding your interests.

Reversed: You are experiencing who you are on a variety of levels. You recognize that you are not just one self, you are many selves. Now, you are being more flexible with ways that you name yourself. It's stimulating to imagine yourself as a variety of different people. Others may not see your multiple selves but you enjoy them.

SEVEN OF CUPS: Emotional Variety and Exploration

Upright: Emotionally, things have been pretty calm for awhile and now you're ready for some excitement. You're seeking new sensations and a variety of emotional experiences. You may want to interact in several relationships or experiment with a variety of feelings within one relationship. You're feeling all of your emotions.

Reversed: You are experiencing variety and activity in your psychic work or in your dreams. The barriers are down between you and others so you may be feeling their emotions. You're exploring your most imaginative fantasies. You are probably expanding and exploring your intuitive abilities and finding new ways to use them. You could also be experimenting with several secret or private relationships.

SEVEN OF SWORDS: Mental Flexibility

Upright: You're experimenting with your schedule, lifestyle, or daily routine. You are exploring and expanding the ways you communicate; you may be talking or writing a great deal! Your lifestyle is full of variety and activity.

Reversed: You're experimenting with your beliefs and attitudes. As you stretch and expand them, you notice how certain beliefs operate in your life and you experiment with changing them or adjusting them to see what new results you get. You may be listening to a variety of internal voices.

SEVEN OF PENTACLES: Physical Experimentation

Upright: You are experimenting with money, material resources, or your body in a variety of ways. You are experiencing the various opportunities that are available as a result of your physical or financial condition. You may be developing some variety in your work or trying out several approaches to money management or investment.

Reversed: You are exploring a variety of ways in which you could feel centered, safe and grounded. You recognize that no one person, thing, or situation can provide you with complete security so now you're experimenting to find new forms of stability and a broader security base.

THE EIGHTS: ORGANIZING

The pictures on the Eights usually show something that is in order. The symbols are placed in a row or a structured pattern. Some sense of priorities has been created by organizing the available elements into a form or structure.

Neutral: With all the Eights, you're organizing yourself and your life. You're carefully, thoughtfully, making choices based on your priorities and on the expansive experiences of the Sevens. You're analyzing or assimilating what you've learned. After you've got everything organized, you'll be able to go on to the integrated flow of the Nine.

Positive: It's a good time to put things in order. It's appropriate to re-evaluate what you're doing and set some priorities for yourself. Go ahead, evaluate your experiences and make some commitments.

Negative: Eights can show that you're over-organized. You may need some more experimental experience (Seven) before you put things in order. Or, it may be time to move on; you might be re-evaluating and re-analyzing things to the extent that you're not living your life, you're analyzing it!

EIGHT OF WANDS: Re-examining the Identity

Upright: You are reflecting on the various roles that you present to others and choosing which ones you want to continue to play. You're establishing some priorities in terms of which roles you're willing to emphasize in your life and which selves (or personalities) you want to de-emphasize.

Reversed: You are sorting out what parts of yourself you want to keep and what parts you want to release. On a private or personal level, you're figuring out what you do and don't like about the way you experience yourself. You're figuring out which parts of your self-image you want to emphasize.

EIGHT OF CUPS: Evaluating Feelings

Upright: You are reflecting on some of your relationships and thinking over what you like and don't like about them. You're putting your emotions into some kind of order and finding ways of categorizing or analyzing your feelings. You are establishing emotional priorities among several relationships or within a single relationship.
Reversed: You're looking at your psychic or intuitive experiences and re-evaluating them. As a result of your experimentation at the Seven level, you're now ready to decide which psychic tools are most appealing to you. You could also be evaluating hidden feelings or a private relationship.

EIGHT OF SWORDS: Organizing Thoughts

Upright: You're actively organizing or reworking something you've said or written. You're looking at your lifestyle and activities and finding ways to re-prioritize what you're doing so that your schedule more closely matches your values. You're examining your communication patterns and making some decisions about which patterns you prefer.

Reversed: You're re-evaluating your beliefs and attitudes and deciding which ones to keep and which ones to toss out. You've had enough experience to know how your beliefs operate. Now, you can pick and choose which ones to emphasize in your life. You may be evaluating how to work with your inner voices and deciding when to attend to each one.

EIGHT OF PENTACLES: Organizing Physical Things

Upright: You are thinking over the style and level of security that you want in your life. You've tried out several different approaches to home, money, or career options and are now ready to reflect on your experiences and make some choices. You're prioritizing your ways of using money, resources, and physical energy. You're making the choices that are necessary in order that your material world will conform more closely to your needs.

Reversed: You're evaluating the different things you've tried in your search for stability. You recognize which processes consistently bring you a deeper level of security. Now, you can re-evaluate your security-seeking patterns and choose the ones that work the best for you.

THE NINES: INTEGRATING

The pictures on the Nines usually show a situation in which little needs to be done in order to keep things working and moving. Since everything is both flexible and in order, the people can almost ignore the situation they're in and things will still proceed and flow.

Neutral: You are experiencing a quality of flow, movement and flexibility. You are smoothly progressing with very little effort or struggle. You have integrated what you experienced and learned in the Sevens and Eights and you now have an ongoing sense of purpose and direction.

Positive: You are experiencing a comfortable and productive flow of energy or resources. You can move along, making steady progress, yet remaining flexible as you go. Go ahead and take advantage of this effortless flow. You are progressing well.

Negative: Your on-going, well-integrated process is disfunctional at this time. Everything seems to be progressing smoothly but it's not to your advantage. You may have established some poor priorities at the Eight level so that what you've integrated isn't really what you want. Or, it may be time to make a choice about future direction (Ten) instead of staying with the current situation.

NINE OF WANDS: The Integrated Self

Upright: You are well-integrated into the roles you're playing and the selves you're presenting to the world. Others see that you are acting naturally and in accordance with your true being. You're making steady progress by being this self. The full range of your personality is revealed as you interact with the world.

Reversed: This is a more internalized flow. You're not locked into one self-image. You can see yourself in a variety of ways without losing a sense of integration or unity. You're experiencing yourself as a person who's flexible and growing.

NINE OF CUPS: Flowing Feelings

Upright: You are really experiencing a flow of emotions. Everything you feel comes easily to the surface and into your awareness. Your relationships are moving and progressively developing. On the emotional plane, you are moving forward with a sense of purpose and direction.

Reversed: Your psychic abilities are functioning smoothly and naturally. Flashes of intuition and inspiration come, unbidden, to the surface. You float in and out of your psychic awareness smoothly, easily, and almost without realizing it. Private feelings or secret relationships are well-integrated into your life.

NINE OF SWORDS: Integrated Thoughts

Upright: Your lifestyle or daily schedule is proceeding smoothly. You can easily and flexibly adjust it when changes are needed without losing sight of your priorities. Verbal or written communication is flowing smoothly and clearly.

Reversed: Your attitudes and opinions are well integrated within your self or your life. You are experiencing the steady, continuous process of watching your beliefs evolve and grow as they work together to form a belief system.

NINE OF PENTACLES: Integrated Security

Upright: Money, resources, and physical energy are moving steadily in your life. The basic financial, career, or home security that you have is flexible and it easily adjusts to changes. You may be experiencing quite a bit of cash flow — equal money coming in and going out. With regard to your health, this shows that your body is functioning in a coordinated, smooth manner.

Reversed: Your security base is solid and can easily adapt to fluctuations. You are feeling more and more stable and secure and at the same time flexible and progressive about the ways you guarantee your safety and groundedness. You have an inner sensation of well-being.

THE TENS: HESITATING

The pictures on the Tens usually show a functioning, working situation that is no longer changing and growing. They show some resistance to making change or taking a risk. Usually the people are looking at what they have already gained with an air of satisfaction or complacency.

Neutral: The question of the Tens is, "are you willing to risk what you have now, to get something that might be better?" Since you're not sure of the answer, you're sitting at the Ten, trying to make up your mind. You have an awareness that your experience could be better or more intense than it is now. You haven't decided if you want to commit to that deeper level of involvement. You're deciding whether to settle for okay, to strive for excellence, or to go for a different experience.

Positive: It's appropriate for you to relax and be satisfied with what you have at the moment. It's not a good idea to push or to challenge yourself at this time. It is appropriate to avoid taking risks and to maintain your own pace.

Negative: You're in danger of stagnating if you don't make a decision soon. You've been avoiding this decision, sitting on the fence, and hedging for too long. It's time to take some action now. You could be trying to make a decision about the future when it's more appropriate to stay with the working system of the Nine. It might also be appropriate to move forward to the excitement of the Page. But, in either case, it's inappropriate to continue hesitating over your decision.

TEN OF WANDS: An Identity Question

Upright: The role you're playing is comfortable and working well but you're aware that it's not changing much anymore. You feel like you're in a rut with your personal growth and direction. It's a comfortable rut so it's hard to make a move to get out of it. Staying at this level for too long will lead to stagnation. You are aware that it is a choice point in your life but for now you're sitting on the fence.

Reversed: You realize that you need to make some choices about the ways you view yourself. You can decide to re-invest in the self-image that you've been affirming or you can take some risks with how you see yourself now and reach for a deeper sense of self-worth.

TEN OF CUPS: An Emotional or Intuitive Crossroads

Upright: A given emotion or relationship has reached the point where it feels very stable, satisfying and safe—but it isn't growing or deepening. You know that you will need to make a decision about whether to continue with this feeling or relationship but you're reluctant, at this point, to make the choice.

Reversed: You've reached a level of security with your psychic work but nothing's changing or growing anymore. You know you need to take some risks and move on but you're not feeling quite ready to do it yet.

TEN OF SWORDS: A Philosophical Choice Point

Upright: Your lifestyle feels very comfortable and safe. Your communication patterns are familiar and easy to maintain because you've been using them for a long time. You're in the process of making some decisions about what to do next regarding lifestyle, schedule, daily routine, or communication, but you're not yet ready to complete the choices and move on. For now, it feels best to avoid a final decision.

Reversed: You have reached a point where you feel comfortable with your beliefs, attitudes, and values. This may lead to a lack of growth in your ideas that could result in mental stagnation. You could choose to stick with the belief system that you've already established and re-commit to it on a deeper level. You could also choose to start over with a whole new set of values. For the moment, you may not clearly know what your choice will be so you're hesitating while you make up your mind.

TEN OF PENTACLES: A Physical Crossroads

Upright: You are recognizing that you may soon need to make some decisions about the kind of security pattern that you have established. Your current security is stable but not growing or developing. Your job or home situation is steady but not stimulating. Your financial situation is safe and low-risk. Pretty soon, things will begin to stagnate if no changes are made. But for now, it feels comfortable to maintain the kind of security that you have and to avoid making too many changes.

Reversed: You have established ways of centering and stabilizing yourself that are working effectively. You know that the time to take risks with your security is approaching but you don't feel ready to take action at this time.

THE PAGES: RISKING

The Page cards usually show a single person, setting out alone on a path. The Pages have an air of faith or confidence about them but they are alone in taking the step. They are usually on foot, with few belongings and little protection. They seem unconcerned about the risks they're taking.

Neutral: With the Pages, you are setting out to take the risks that you've contemplated or avoided in the Tens. You are daring to re-commit to something or invest energy in something that you hope and feel will pan out. You're jumping off the high dive but you don't know for sure what's at the bottom. You have all the experiences of Ace through Ten behind you, so your risk is a calculated one but there are no guarantees!

Positive: It's appropriate or even advisable to take some risks and stick your neck out a little. Jump in and try it because it will probably pay off.

Negative: In this situation, risk-taking is inappropriate. It could be that your tendency to leap before you look is getting in your way. You might need to be more cautious. It's also possible that you're stuck in the adventure of risk-taking; it's time to use the focus of the Knight.

PAGE OF WANDS: Taking Identity Risks

Upright: You're taking risks with a particular role you've played. You may be exhibiting a part of yourself that you've previously hidden. You're daring to present yourself, publicly, in a way that may feel a bit scary. You are optimistic that the result will be worth the risk but aware that there are no guarantees.

Reversed: You are taking the risk of privately naming or viewing yourself in a way that might change your life considerably. The old self-image was fine, as far as it went, but it was limited. Now, you're determined to be all you can be and daring to see yourself as a more adventuresome person.

PAGE OF CUPS: Emotional Risk-Taking

Upright: You're taking some emotional risks in a public, up-front way. You've chosen to jump in and commit to an emotional direction or relationship even though you're not sure where it will lead. You may have had a relationship that was working pretty well on a certain level. Now, you want to make it better than "okay." You're willing to risk losing what already exists in order to create what it could become. It may feel a little scary but you have some confidence that it will succeed.

Reversed: You're taking some risks with your psychic abilities and allowing them to lead you into some exciting but somewhat scary directions. You may be allowing yourself to go deeper into your meditation or take action on some intuitive flashes that seem pretty wild. You don't know where these psychic paths might take you but you're willing to go for it. You could also be daring to examine your hidden or feared emotions.

PAGE OF SWORDS: Risks in Thoughts or Lifestyle

Upright: You are taking some risks with your lifestyle or daily routine, daring to commit to some ideas that you've been avoiding up to now.

You are taking some risks with communicating things you have been holding back, or with communicating in a way that feels scary to you. You're willing to take risks in order to actively pursue and manifest a philosophy or value system that's important to you.

Reversed: You're daring to commit to some beliefs and attitudes that involve growth and risk. You are mentally pushing your philosophy to its ultimate conclusions. You are willing to take the risk of losing the comfort of previous beliefs for the sake of establishing more meaningful values. You may also be daring to communicate with your inner voices in a new way.

PAGE OF PENTACLES: Security Risks

Upright: You are making a renewed commitment to a security base that seemed on the brink of stagnation. Putting more physical energy, resources or money into this project may seem a little risky but you have some faith that it will work out. There is an awareness that you may be re-investing in something that has passed its peak but also a sense of confidence that it's worth a try. You are taking some calculated risks with the physical things that represent material security for you. You're going for the Olympics instead of settling for "high school star."

Reversed: You're taking risks with some things that have always made you feel safe and secure in the past. You're willing to risk those things for the sake of more aliveness and a deeper, more mature sense of security or stability. You may realize that your security has been safe, but somewhat superficial, in the past; now you're ready to explore some possibilities that could be more fulfilling.

THE KNIGHTS: FOCUSING

The images of the Knights are almost always figures with covered heads. Their armor encourages them to look in one limited direction. They are often riding horses which are rushing straight ahead or facing a chosen path. The Knight's body may also be covered or protected by armor or weapons, showing imperviousness to attack. The Knight is totally determined to proceed according to plan.

Neutral: All the Knights reflect intensity and focus. When a Knight appears, you are experiencing single-mindedness in some part of your life. You are bringing all your efforts to bear on a particular thing, in order to give it the advantage of your complete attention.

Positive: You've needed to really sink your teeth into something and you get a feeling of satisfaction from being so intensely involved. It's appropriate for you to focus attention in this area.

Negative: You're wearing blinders. Here, the Knight can show that you're being too dogmatic, fixed or narrow in your approach. You need to lighten up a little. To be so intensely focused at this time is disfunctional. It may be appropriate to go back and take some more risks (Page) or to move forward into a more relaxed, mature expression of your interests (Queen).

KNIGHT OF WANDS: Focusing on the Self

Upright: You are focusing intensely on playing the role you've chosen for yourself. You are intently presenting a particular part of you to the world. You're so determined to be that self that you may seem self-centered. You're bringing all your attention to bear on your self and

70

your self-expression.

Reversed: After taking some personal risks, you may be feeling the need to put intense energy into being with yourself and discovering your self. You're so committed to your own growth and direction that you may be unaware of the rest of the world. You may be strongly introverted now, or you may be exploring a part of your personality in a secret or hidden manner.

KNIGHT OF CUPS: Emotional or Intuitive Focus

Upright: You are completely involved in an emotional sensation. You're so involved in this feeling or relationship that everything else seems insignificant by comparison. In fact, all other relationships and emotions may be blocked by this one.

Reversed: You are focusing on your psychic or spiritual awareness. You may be spending all your time meditating or tuning in to your inner processes. Much of your attention may be given over to your dreams and unconscious-level activities. You could be totally focused on a particular psychic or intuitive direction to the exclusion of other possibilities. Or, you could be conducting an all-consuming, but clandestine, relationship or harboring a private but intense emotion.

KNIGHT OF SWORDS: Philosophical Focus

Upright: You are deeply committed to acting out your philosophical ideals in your daily lifestyle. You are so involved with the pattern of your daily routine that everything else seems to recede in importance. You are completely focused on your intellect, and on using your mind and ideas. You have a strong desire to express what you think and you are intent on communicating your ideas to others.

Reversed: You're putting incredible energy into supporting or examining a particular set of beliefs or attitudes. You may be focused on supporting and reinforcing your own values as you choose to reject

71

others' values. You're intensely involved with private communication, between parts of yourself or between yourself and others.

KNIGHT OF PENTACLES: Focused in the Material World

Upright: You are focusing so hard on establishing security that nothing else seems relevant. You may seem like a workaholic. You are putting all your energy into your home, career, physical body, or financial affairs. You are feeling that you need to work hard right now, with few distractions.

Reversed: Here, you're putting all your energy and attention into feeling safe, secure and centered. You have recently taken some risks with your psychological sense of groundedness and now you're becoming centered on a deeper level.

THE QUEENS: FULFILLING

The Queens are usually shown as women who are sitting solidly on thrones, clearly in positions of power and authority. Of course men, as well as women, can reach this level of growth and maturity so we need to be conscious of the fact that the Queens represent concepts, not gender.

Neutral: All the Queens represent competency. They show that you've achieved a deep level of fulfillment, skill, or maturity. Usually, others recognize this quality in you and you are given the respect or status that's due to you.

Positive: You have indeed achieved a high level of skill or maturity. Your competence is one of your strongest assets right now. You can move through your life with authority and strength, adjusting yourself when it's necessary, directing others when that's appropriate.

Negative: You've reached such a high level of competency that you're isolated from others. You don't fit into society or a particular group because you've out-stretched them. No one else is at your level. It can be a little lonely at the top! It may be time to use the intensity of the Knight to put your energy into something that challenges and stimulates you. Or, it may be time to move on and let go with the King.

QUEEN OF WANDS: A Mature Identity

Upright: You've reached a high level of personal integrity and maturity within the role you're playing. You are clear on who you are and nothing can take that from you. You are self-confident in most all situations. You are content with your general process of growth and you have a sense of continuing development. A feeling of maturity and confidence radiates from you as you function in this role or identity.

Reversed: You have reached a high level of self-respect. No one else may realize it but you are self-assured. This card can indicate that people within a limited group appreciate who you are. You are pretty self-sufficient and recognize and accept your own independence.

QUEEN OF CUPS: Emotional or Intuitive Maturity

Upright: Your interpersonal interaction is highly evolved and fulfilling. You experience your emotions deeply and allow others to feel theirs. You are skilled at processing your feelings and understanding what is happening in your relationships. You express a deep empathy and understanding toward others. You have reached a strong level of maturity and depth with a relationship or emotion.

Reversed: Your psychic or intuitive abilities are well-developed and may feel like second nature to you. You have reached some level of maturity and competency in dealing with your unconscious awareness. You can rely on your intuitive inspiration.

QUEEN OF SWORDS: Intellectual Maturity

Upright: Your mental faculties are well-tuned. You are expressing your philosophy, fully and powerfully, through your lifestyle and activities. You are not likely to be threatened by other peoples' lifestyles because you are sure of your own. Your communication process is strong and effective; you are powerful in presenting your ideas because you understand them so thoroughly.

Reversed: You have been involved with a particular set of attitudes or beliefs for a long time. There is depth and maturity to the way you understand what you believe. You've worked out the kinks in what you believe to be "true" about life and are now confident that your values will hold true no matter what comes your way. You communicate with yourself at a rich and meaningful level.

QUEEN OF PENTACLES: Physical Competence

Upright: Your hard work has paid off in a high level of competence and security. You have a skill that you can use to earn income at any time. Your abilities are recognized and documented. You may have reached a point in your physical health where a particular pattern of health (or ill health) has become totally integrated into your body. Your home, career, or financial security are established.

Reversed: You know how to create and maintain the kind of personal security you want. You are centered within yourself and the upsets of life are unlikely to throw you off balance. This could also indicate that you have a well-developed talent or skill that you are not currently employing in your life.

74

THE KINGS: RELEASING

Most of the King cards show men, enthroned, in poses similar to those of the Queens. As with the queens, it's important to remember that the concept of king-ness exists outside of gender. There is often a feeling of finality or completion to the Kings. In some decks, they are even positioned so that they are looking or moving away from the rest of the cards, facing a new future.

Neutral: The Kings appear when you are closing out patterns and releasing the past; You are completing or ending what has gone before because it no longer works for you. Only when you release the old will you be ready for the future. You realize that the end is just as important as the beginning and that you want to value it. You can show your respect by making a clean break and performing a symbolic, letting-go, ritual.

Positive: You're wise to reach closure on an old pattern that's no longer effective in your life. If you decide to perform some kind of symbolic ritual to signify the letting-go process, you can reach a satisfying state of completion. With all due appreciation for the past, it's time to let it go.

Negative: It's not appropriate to be letting go of the past yet. You're not really ready for completion or closure on that part of your life. Maybe you still have something to learn or something to give to the old situation. It's not yet time to release it. It's also possible that you've already moved forward, to a new Ace. Fixating on releasing the past is not appropriate.

KING OF WANDS: Releasing an Old Identity

Upright: You've gotten as much value as you can out of the old identity and now it's time to let it go. You may want to perform some public act that shows others that you are moving away from your former self. You've explored the old identity as much as possible, worked with it, changed it, and developed it to the point where nothing more can be done with it. You've reached the end of a phase of personal development.

Reversed: You're letting go of an old self-image. Regardless of how others have seen you, you've had a particular image of yourself that it's time to end. You may want to do a private ritual to symbolically release the old familiar self that doesn't feel like you anymore.

KING OF CUPS: Releasing an Emotional Pattern

Upright: An emotion has run its course and is no longer operative in your life. This could mean that a relationship is ending completely or that a particular part of the relationship is ending. The old pattern has become a habit that is no longer meaningful or satisfying. Nothing can be done now to retain or reclaim the vigor of the original feelings. You need to make some real or symbolic gesture that shows you've reached a point of closure or completion around this feeling or relationship. You may need to fully experience your grief and mourn its passing.

Reversed: An involvement with a psychic process has reached an end. You've reached the completion of a phase in your psychic or spiritual growth. You could be leaving a church or spiritual group or ending a time of disbelief in psychic phenomena. It's important that you symbolize this rite of passage in a way that's meaningful to you.

KING OF SWORDS: Releasing an Old Lifestyle or Idea

Upright: Old philosophical ideas have finally exhausted themselves. It's time to trade them in for a new point of view. Your habitual communication pattern is no longer appropriate for your life; it's time for a change. You may need to complete some communication with someone. You may have reached an end in a training or learning period.

You know that your old lifestyle is no longer meaningful or interesting to you; it's time to take some definite action to reach closure on the old activities.

Reversed: You're letting go of some old beliefs and values that no longer seem appropriate to you. You're now ready to stop living by those old beliefs . . . they're not working anyway. An inner voice may have outlived its usefulness in your life; it's time to release or transform it.

KING OF PENTACLES: Releasing Something Physical

Upright: This shows an end to a physical, material, or financial pattern in your life. There is no point in re-committing resources, physical energy, or money to this project. It is important to recognize that your investment in this security pattern has run its course. It is time to take some action to end the old pattern, and withdraw from your involvement in that direction.

Reversed: The security pattern that you're in now has become so limiting and rigid that it no longer works for you. The things that used to make you feel grounded and safe are no longer effective or perhaps, no longer necessary. There's no point in continuing with the old "security blanket." Let it go.

6

THE MAJOR ARCANA

The Major Arcana cards represent the great concepts of the Universe. Each card shows us one theme, lesson, message, or basic energy. We all work with these themes in our lives according to our own growth processes. As you explore the meanings of the Major Arcana cards, be conscious of the multiple ways in which you could experience these concepts in your life. Be aware that each energy can be used appropriately or to excess. None of them are "good" or "bad" energies and all of them can be used in productive or non-productive ways.

Each of the Major Arcana cards has a name and an assigned Roman Numeral. Most authors agree on the Roman Numeral designations for the Major cards; the biggest area of disagreement seems to be in numbering Strength and Justice. In this book, I am assigning Strength to VIII and Justice to XI. You will need to check your own deck to see which way it is numbered. It is convenient to have the Roman Numeral designations of the cards since the descriptive names of the cards are more frequently changed. Many authors have renamed Major Arcana cards so that the names reflect their interpretations of the cards. The names I have given below are the standard names though they are not necessarily the names I would choose for my own deck. Most of the names are either masculine or feminine and the pictures reflect men or women accordingly. As you know, I do not feel that the cards

78

have any relationship to a person's gender. Anyone can be or experience any of the Major Arcana cards.

For each Major Arcana card, I have included a description of the most common images. This is a somewhat limited description since each deck will tend to reflect the cards' energies in its own way. I have included the neutral, positive, and negative interpretations for each card as well as the upright and reversed applications.

THE FOOL - 0

In most decks, the Fool is shown as a person who is confidently setting out on a journey with only a few necessities in a small bag. The person is often blindfolded to indicate that the future is not clear or visible. The gender of the person may also be unclear, making it easier to identify the Fool with people of either sex. Sometimes the Fool is about to step off a cliff into nothingness, but the facial expression is still confident and trusting. In many decks a dog is either guarding the way or pulling the person back from the cliff. The dog represents the protection that the Fool experiences.

Neutral: You are experiencing absolute faith and trust in the Universe. You have no sense of worry or fear and no awareness that worry or fear could even exist. You have a feeling of protection and a sense that everything will work out. You may be a little naive and innocent and you are open to whatever the future brings.

Positive: Go forth in faith; be more trusting. You'll be protected in your innocence as you follow your heart's desire.

Negative: You're operating too much on blind faith. You need to check out the facts a little more and become more realistic about what's happening. You may need to take more action instead of just having faith. You may be too naive or trusting.

Upright: Having faith in external events, in other people, and in the world at large, you are confidently taking action.

Reversed: This signifies having faith in yourself, Universal wisdom, or your inner guidance.

THE MAGICIAN - I

In a magic show, we know that what's real to the Magician may not be what's real to the audience. The Magician, familiar with tricks of the trade, can discriminate between illusion and truth while the audience may not know the difference. The Tarot Magician, usually a man, is sometimes shown with traditional magician's tools though, in most decks, these are replaced with the symbols of the Minor Arcana suits. The processes of the Minor Arcana are the tools that the Magician uses in order to move between the worlds of fantasy and reality. The Magician shows us that we ourselves can use our intellects, our feelings, our personal strengths, and talents and our practical skills in order to move between those two worlds.

Neutral: The Magician appears when you are aware that several different perceptions of reality exist. You are able to understand and describe the various points of view. You might also be discriminating between reality and fantasy, among two or more fantasies, or among two or more realities.

Positive: Your ability to discriminate among your various realities, between reality and illusion, or between your view and someone else's view is valuable right now. You have all the tools available to do so. Go ahead and clarify the differences between various perceptions of reality.

Negative: You're trying too hard to discriminate between fantasy and reality. You're being too picky and losing sight of the whole by focusing too much on the parts. You're keeping the two worlds too separated. Right now, it may be appropriate for all the differences to exist without delineating them. Some blend or clarity will come in the end; for now, it's not appropriate to try to figure out what's real and what isn't.

Upright: Your personal reality is not the same as the collective reality. Your experience of a situation is unique, different from another's, or different from the group's experience. You can discriminate between the factors in the current situation which represent the consensus point of view and those that reflect your own perspective. Events and conditions in the outer world need to be sorted out. Your experience of a relationship, a job, a family, or even the weather, is different than that of the other(s) involved.

Reversed: You are discriminating between your personal fantasies and your own experience of reality. You're observing what's happening in your life and comparing that reality with your fantasy of what you wish were happening. You might also be contrasting and comparing the various realities that are experienced as 'true' by different parts of you. You're looking at your dreams and visions and deciding which ones you want to manifest into reality and which are better left as fantasies.

THE HIGH PRIESTESS - II

The High Priestess is most often a woman, shown seated at the gates of a temple, with a veil around her head, a book in her hand, and a serene facial expression. She is at the gateway between this world and another, more spiritual world. The veil, the door, and the book all represent the boundaries between the two worlds that need to be crossed in order to experience spiritual enlightenment or psychic understanding.

Neutral: The High Priestess represents awareness of the greater self — the self that spans realities, exists in many planes, and is part of the stuff of the Universe. You are in tune with that boundless self, the spiritual part of the self. You have a need to ignore the distractions and limitations of the physical world (step over the boundaries into another reality) to tune in to that expanded self. You may appear to be aloof and removed from the world and from others. You are communing with your higher self.

Positive: Attunement is needed now. It could be valuable for you to set aside worldly worries and meditate or become unified with a larger, more Universal consciousness.

Negative: You're getting too much into your meditative world. You are too isolated and removed from others or from the material world.

Upright: Your meditation or attunement is taking a conscious, even physically observable form. You may literally be removed from the activities of your day-to-day life, in retreat or in your own space, while you tune in to your inner voice and spiritual awareness.

Reversed: You are tuning in to the Universe on a private level. People may not even be aware that you're doing it. They may vaguely sense that you're not quite all "here" but they aren't sure why. You may not be meditating in an obvious way but you are finding a personal way of tuning in and becoming more aware of your spiritual wholeness.

THE EMPRESS - III

The Empress is usually shown as a rounded, warm, and caring woman. Her environment is one of abundance; grains have been harvested, herbs are available for healing. She has both the emotional and physical resources for healing, feeding, and nurturing people.

Neutral: You are giving deep and total love and nurturing. Something or someone needs to be loved, protected, and healed. You are sensitive to the physical and emotional needs of yourself and others and you are in a position to meet those needs and heal wounds. You are highly dedicated to the nurturing, caretaking process.

Positive: It's appropriate or even necessary to be involved with healing and nurturing now. You have the strength and awareness to protect or heal yourself or others. Go ahead and do it.

Negative: You are trying to heal, nurture, or protect someone who doesn't need it or want it right now. You may be draining yourself of energy by taking care of yourself or others. The method of caretaking may be inappropriate. You are probably being over-protective, preventing yourself or another from taking necessary risks. You may need to stop playing the caretaker role.

Upright: You are nurturing someone else. The nurturing can take a very obvious or tangible form. This could involve giving a massage, holding someone, bringing over chicken soup, or leaving someone alone if that's what she needs. It could also take the form of giving someone loving energy in an intangible form. The card implies that you are aware of what she needs and able to give it to her.

Reversed: You are nurturing yourself. You are taking time to cozy up and treat yourself well. This may mean taking time out, reading a good book, feeding yourself, or taking a hot bath. It could also mean loving and healing yourself on a more psychological level.

THE EMPEROR - IV

The Emperor is most often depicted as a man with obvious worldly power. The figure of authority, he sits on his throne and surveys all he has conquered. He is an executive, a leader who has risen to the top because he has been aggressive and willing to put all his energy into the climb. There is no clear dividing line between him and his empire—he IS the empire.

Neutral: You have committed yourself to identifying with a force that has a great deal of power in the world. In fact, you may have chosen to give up some of your individuality or differentness in order to identify with this power. Since you have made a commitment to rising or falling according to the success of that power, it's to your advantage to energize and support it.

Positive: You have a need to identify with the powerful force or group and lose some of your isolation and separateness. You can gain a degree of comfort, satisfaction, or success by associating with this strong and established force. You may need to give someone temporary power in your life if you're at a time when you don't feel able to make healthy choices for yourself. Go ahead and give up some of your freedom to become allied with the force at hand.

Negative: You're giving up too much of your own freedom or power in order to identify with a (seemingly) more powerful force. You're losing your separateness and that is a problem for you. You won't personally be satisfied if you identify with this power structure.

Upright: You have a vested interest in a particular culture, social group, institution, economic group, company, or community. You identify with a powerful group or individual. You may attend meetings, go to work, or participate in family or social activities that identify you as "one of them." Because you identify with this person or group, your success or failure in the world is affected by theirs.

Reversed: One part of your personality, one need, desire, or drive controls or dominates the rest of you. This could be an emotion, attitude, belief, or philosophy which overrides everything else in your life and completely dictates and directs your actions, successes, and failures.

THE HIEROPHANT - V

The image of the Hierophant is usually that of a religious leader, often the Pope. He is a morally conscious and conscientious person who has the desire and responsibility for blessing others or making decisions for others.

Neutral: You have chosen to align yourself with a particular philosophy or group and you feel a great deal of loyalty to it. You are conscientious about living out the philosophy in your daily life and aware of measuring and choosing your actions and behavior based on it. You are willing to take on responsibility in order to support the philosophy. At the same time, you are accountable to the philosophy and you judge yourself by it. You could be free to disentangle yourself from this involvement at any time: you choose to be involved.

Positive: You're establishing a relationship with a philosophy that can really lead and direct your life. It's a good idea to go ahead and take responsibility for behaving in accordance with this ethical system. You can assume leadership since you are loyal to your ideals and accountable for your actions.

Negative: You're probably being too accountable to your beliefs or philosophy. You may be excessively concerned with making your life the perfect reflection of your ideals. You may be assuming too much responsibility for making decisions that are based on your what you think you "should" do. You may be limiting or harming yourself by your loyalty to a belief system or philosophy that isn't healthy for you right now.

Upright: You are involved with a group or another person because of your shared philosophy, common goals, or social orientation. You may have a sense of connectedness with a family, lover, church, political group, spiritual group, or whatever. You feel loyalty toward these others and choose to live in accordance with the beliefs you share with them. You may even have a position of leadership within the group. The group acts as your inspiration, encouraging you to truly live up to your beliefs. It may also act as your judge, letting you know when you're off the track.

Reversed: A part of yourself is accountable to another part of yourself. You are choosing to live by a particular philosophy or belief structure that seems important to you. As a result, you direct your own actions in accordance with your philosophy. Even when your drives or desires may lead you in one direction, you will choose to curb them in order to be accountable to your larger goals or aims.

THE LOVERS - VI

The image on the Lovers card usually shows two individuals who are being brought together by a third force (animal or person) that represents the need for unity. The third force may be a benevolent being or a threatening dragon but in either case it encourages the two people to come together.

Neutral: You are involved in the process of cooperation. Two or more forces or people in your life have joined together in coalition because they are working for a common goal. The forces will probably never become one unit, they may not work together in all ways, but they do combine energies for a general or specific purpose.

Positive: Two or more forces in your life are working together in a constructive and productive relationship. People, ideas, or activities are cooperating in a coordinated manner. This interaction validates and supports you as well as the others involved because you are working jointly toward goals that you all value.

Negative: Two or more incompatible elements or individuals are coming together. You may be trying to forcefully create an impossible relationship between factors or people whose goals and interests do not mesh. They really can't be expected to cooperate with each other.

Upright: You are working together, in coalition with others, to accomplish some joint goal. You may not agree on anything else, but, for this purpose, you'll come together and work cooperatively.

Reversed: One part of you is cooperating with another part of you. You may hold some beliefs and attitudes that don't always work smoothly together. Here, you are finding a way to bring them together and have them support each other— you may realize that you can be both fat and beautiful!

THE CHARIOT - VII

The Chariot card is represented by a person, usually male, riding in a chariot that is drawn by two horses, cats, or mythical beasts. The Chariot may be moving at an incredible speed but the driver looks calm because he is attuned to the beasts and the fast motion.

Neutral: You are totally in tune with a fast-moving process or event. You are aware of the tolerances and limitations of the situation and you know, instinctively, how to act and react in order to direct or affect the movement from within. You are not standing outside the situation; you can't control it from outside. By immersing yourself in it, you have become part of it and are therefore able to direct its course.

Positive: Events are moving quickly but you understand the situation well enough to know, instinctively, how to act or react. You know how to handle yourself within the situation, so go ahead and immerse yourself in the current transition or growth process. The more you are involved with the energies and harmonies of the changes, the better you'll be able to use and direct them.

Negative: Becoming immersed in the rapid pace of change and transition creates stress and tension for you right now. Things may be moving too fast for you. Being in the midst of it is not the best way to direct events. You need to get outside of the situation.

Upright: You are in a situation where transition is occurring at an amazing rate. You are completely involved and attuned to the fast pace of the changes that are happening in your relationship, home, career, or worldly situation. You sensitively shift, balance, and react to participate in keeping things moving.

Reversed: Your own beliefs, attitudes, or emotions are changing and transforming at a rapid rate. You are so involved with these changes that you don't feel like you're consciously controlling them. In fact, the more attuned you are to the transition process, the more you're able to maneuver and direct it.

STRENGTH - VIII

The Strength card usually shows a person who is in tune with the animal forces. It may be represented by a woman who is embracing a lion; it could also be a male weight-lifter, displaying his muscles and physical strength. The person is not afraid of the animal power; she is appreciative of its strength and its will to survive. (In some decks, this card may be numerically interchanged with the XI card—Justice.)

Neutral: You are experiencing the gut-level, instinctive drives that you rely on for your protection or survival. You may feel as though you are fighting for your life. You are responding to a force that is not logical, and not even intuitive: it is just a compelling drive. It seems like a biological, emotional, or spiritual survival mechanism that has been triggered without your conscious awareness.

Positive: The compelling drives that you feel right now are there for your protection and well-being. They support your continued efforts to survive and take care of yourself. You might not be clear about why you're doing this but it's important to follow your impulses.

Negative: You are experiencing a compulsive behavior or feeling that is not necessary. You may be responding to a situation in a particular, defensive manner because that's how you needed to respond in the past in order to survive. The current situation probably doesn't merit that intense, compulsive response. Your compulsions are habit patterns or addictions that are no longer beneficial to you.

Upright: This may indicate an obvious, physical, compelling force.

Something outside you is strongly urging you to take a certain action. You may feel irresistibly drawn to a particular person or you may be struggling to create a farm in rocky soil. Your fierce determination to pursue your goal doesn't seem logical but does seem irrefutable.

Reversed: You are experiencing intense inner drives that compel you to act in a particular way. You are behaving in a way that seems illogical but is actually in tune with your own biological or emotional needs. You may be struggling for emotional survival in a situation that seems abusive or threatening to you.

THE HERMIT - IX

The Hermit is most often shown as an older person, usually a man, who is standing in a high or isolated space, carrying a lantern, and looking down at a scene that is illuminated by the lantern. He seems to embody the qualities of wisdom, illumination, and clear vision.

Neutral: You are temporarily withdrawing from others or from your normal environment in order to get some perspective on your situation. You feel that you have gathered enough data and information and you have enough personal wisdom to sort things out on your own. You feel that you want to analyze or understand your role within your relationship, group, job, family, or whatever. Once you have become clear within yourself, you intend to return to the situation and play a more satisfying or effective role within it.

Positive: It's time for retreat. You need to separate yourself from others and from your routine activities in order to gain some perspective on them. You have, within you, all the knowledge and wisdom you need in order to understand what has been happening. Now, you just need to take the time to think things through before you rejoin the group.

Negative: Separation from your regular activities and friends is a problem for you at this time. By removing yourself from others, you are depriving yourself of the perspective that they can give you. You really don't have enough information to figure things out alone.

Upright: You are involved in an actual physical withdrawal from your usual life. you may be going out of town for the weekend, locking yourself in your room, or otherwise showing people that you want to be alone to gain some perspective on your life.

Reversed: You are withdrawing within yourself to think things through: You may be going through the motions of your everyday activities but, emotionally, you have withdrawn. You feel this is necessary in order for you to sort things out alone.

THE WHEEL OF FORTUNE - X

The Wheel of Fortune is some kind of wheel or circle that is spinning through space or lodging at a stopping point. If any people are pictured, they are on or within the wheel, powerless to change its course.

Neutral: The Wheel shows that something has been triggered or started that will roll, through a natural course of events, to its appropriate resting place. You have done everything that can be done to get things moving. You have initiated some action: the ball has been played, the applications have been sent, the questions have been asked, the mat ter has been set in motion—the roulette wheel has been spun. There is nothing more that you can do. You are waiting to see how others, or the Universal energies, respond.

Positive: Everything possible has been done, by you or by others, to set things in motion, so you need not push yourself any harder. Simply relax and wait to see what the Universe sends in response.

Negative: You've set something in motion that you can no longer control. There isn't anything you can do to stop the action, short of dramatic interference (like overturning the roulette table!). Unless you are willing to take drastic measures, you'll just have to wait and see where things end up—it feels like a problem but there's nothing more you can do about it.

Upright: You've set events in motion in a concrete, observable way. You have actually sent a letter, called someone, or made travel reservations. You've done something, in the real world, to get things started.

Reversed: You've set things in motion through your wishes or affirmations. You may not have done anything that anyone can observe, but you've set things rolling in your mind. You may have sent a mental or emotional plea to the Universe and now you're waiting for a response.

JUSTICE - XI

The Justice card usually reflects the establishment of some sort of balance, equilibrium, or justice. A scale, judge, or decision-maker may be shown—all of these are supposed to represent fairness and perfect balance. Sometimes the judge holds a sword to show that the just decision is backed by a powerful force or authority. (This card may be numerically interchanged with Strength—VIII.)

Neutral: You are establishing equilibrium or balance in your life. You recognize that, in our Universe, no state is permanent: a natural process of action and reaction occurs. Like a pendulum that has been pulled too far to one side, you are naturally swinging in the opposite direction. You have have done something to an extreme, now you are doing something else in order to balance it out. You may balance work with play, sadness with joy, and so forth. The present situation, whatever it is, will pass and be balanced out by its opposite.

Positive: It's appropriate to establish equilibrium. Understanding all sides of the issue at hand, you can play a role in keeping things balanced. You can be fair to all points of view. You may be in the process of establishing a balance between two polarized factions or issues

Negative: Creating equilibrium, balance, and fairness is a problem for you right now. If the pendulum has been swinging in one direction, the reverse swing may create some difficulties for you. You may be bending over backwards to be fair to others at some cost to yourself. Or, you may be pushing your luck—be aware of the backswing!

Upright: You are creating an observable balance of power, energy, or material possessions between yourself and others. You may also be creating balance among others—doing some arbitration for them.

Reversed: You are creating a balance within your own life. If you've been very serious, maybe you're lightening up a bit. Or, if you've been very publicly active, maybe you're becoming more of a recluse. Your bodily processes could be seeking a state of equilibrium—they could be swinging from one extreme to another. You're concerned with achieving some kind of psychological or internal balance in your life.

THE HANGED MAN - XII

The Hanged Man is a person, usually a man, hanging upside down. (You may need to look twice to check out whether it's upright or reversed!) In most cases, his facial expression is calm and peaceful; there is no sense of death or distress about the picture. You get the feeling that the person could jump down, whole and hearty, and continue on the path at any moment.

Neutral: The Hanged Man is a card of timing and effectiveness. There is a sense of waiting for the appropriate time, situation, or circumstances. You are aware of what you want to do and you may even be conscious of the next move or direction, but you are also aware that things are not quite set for action yet. You may be watching others act. You may sense that you are seeing things from another perspective but you aren't interfering in their activities. You are hanging around, suspended in mid-air, waiting to make the next move. You will act when the time and circumstances are right.

Positive: It's a good idea to wait for a better time in which to make your move. You know what you want to do. Now, just watch for the appropriate opportunity, energy, or situation to manifest. Then you can, and will, take action.

Negative: You're waiting for the perfect time, person, or circumstances. Your dream of that perfect time is a little unrealistic and if you keep waiting for it, you may never act. Waiting for a "better opportunity" is inappropriate right now. No more procrastinating!

Upright: You're waiting for external circumstances to be right. When the right job, person, house, or situation comes along, you'll take action. You know that you'll recognize the cues and be ready to move as soon as you see them.

Reversed: You're waiting for yourself to be ready. External circumstances may or may not be perfect but that doesn't matter. What matters is whether you're ready, inside, to take this step. When you're in the right frame of mind, or emotionally prepared, you'll take action.

DEATH - XIII

The Death card often arouses quite a reaction in people who've never seen a Tarot deck before. It usually displays a grim reaper, a skeleton, or some other representation of physical death. Some Tarot readers do interpret the card quite literally as physical death—some even remove the card from their decks. However, most people use a more symbolic interpretation of the card.

Neutral: You are experiencing a total change, transformation, or metamorphosis. The pressures in the current situation are becoming so strong that you are actually choosing to change things. You need to destroy the old in order to generate something new out of its ashes. You are regenerating something, getting to the heart of the matter and totally transforming it. Superficial changes no longer seem to be enough: The old situation needs to be turned inside out.

Positive: You're ready for a total change in your life. You want to experience the metamorphosis and will gain maximum benefit from it. An old pattern or situation is being destroyed to make room for something brand new—a caterpillar is becoming a butterfly.

Negative: You may be destroying something unnecessarily. Perhaps there is no accompanying rebirth or creation. You are not ready for intense change on that deep and total level. You're better prepared to rest and assimilate what you've already done, not to go through the demanding process of death and rebirth.

Upright: The material circumstances of your life are going through a monumental transformation. Your body, house, career, relationship, and/or lifestyle may be undergoing a tremendous, observable metamorphosis.

Reversed: You are going through an emotional or personal regeneration process. Your circumstances may not be changing at all, but inside you are completely transforming. You may be sensing a total psychological death and rebirth. You are destroying one way of being so that a new way can be born.

TEMPERANCE - XIV

Temperance is often portrayed by a person, usually female, pouring something back and forth between two goblets. The substance might be a liquid or a form of energy. By combining and blending what's in the cups, something new is formed and created. There is usually an indication of divine inspiration in the card. The cups show that the elements being blended could come from an unconscious or psychic source.

Neutral: You are blending diverse elements to create something new.

You combine the many elements, allowing them to affect and transform each other. No one element dominates. Together they mesh and blend into a new whole. You are aware that the whole is truly greater than the sum of its parts.

Positive: You are using your particular creative talents to the maximum. It's appropriate for you to be combining materials, resources, people, or ideas into beautiful and wonderful new forms.

Negative: You're blending things together that won't stay blended. You're trying to mix oil and water—or you're adding so much color to your paint palette that you're just getting mud color. It may be that your creation is already completed and you're still trying to make it better. At the moment, you'd be better off to let well enough alone. It could also be that it's just not appropriate for you to be creative right now. Maybe you need to turn your attention to other areas of your life.

Upright: You are blending tangible, physical elements or factors to make new wholes. You may be an artist, alchemist, baker, party-giver, or grass-roots organizer. You're using your special talents to creatively produce a tangible product.

Reversed: You're blending parts of yourself or your life together into a new form. YOU are your art form; your life is your canvas. You may also be blending or combining psychic or psychological elements into new forms.

THE DEVIL - XV

The Devil card often provokes as strong a response as the Death card, especially from those who've been raised in the Christian tradition. The image is sometimes the traditional "devil" with red skin, horns and tail, sometimes a person, and often a half-animal, half-human being. Usually, the Devil is restricting people from moving or acting freely. The Devil card usually reflects whatever symbolizes traps or limitations to its author. It's important to note that the Horned God of Paganism is probably the model for the Devil. Its undeserved bad reputation undoubtedly stems from the Church's efforts to demonstrate that the Pagan religion would trap people and keep them from "true enlightenment."

Neutral: The Devil does show that you are experiencing some boundaries and limits in your life. You are seeing that your options and choices are being narrowed and your life is becoming more structured and somewhat less flexible. By making certain assumptions or establishing baseline conditions, you are ruling out some of your options.

Positive: You are choosing to create some positive and supportive boundaries and limits in your life. The structures you're creating are solid foundations for your future growth and development. By making some assumptions and clear choices now, you're arriving at a manageable and effective course of action. The surrounding walls or boundaries are providing a space in which you can focus your energy and become centered.

Negative: The limitations and boundaries in your life have become a trap. You have narrowed your options to the point where the only choices available are harmful or unappealing to you. Things that you thought would function as solid, secure foundations and support systems have now become cages. You need to begin looking for new options—your old assumptions are no longer healthy for you.

Upright: Something in the environment is narrowing your options. Someone else is creating a structure or pattern in your life that limits your choices. A physical, financial, emotional, or intellectual situation is creating boundaries and structures for you.

Reversed: Your own attitudes, beliefs, and assumptions are creating boundaries and structures in your life. You are establishing certain conditions in your life that limit you from behaving in a particular way. You are making some personal or internal decisions that automatically rule out some choices and leave others open.

THE TOWER - XVI

The Tower shows a building that is tumbling to the ground and collapsing. It may have been struck by lightning; people may be falling out of it. There is the feeling of a disaster in progress. The force has already struck the building but the resultant chaos has not run its course, the final settling has not taken place.

Neutral: You have decided to change a basic or core belief in your life. Because you have believed certain things, those things have manifested in your life as foundations upon which your life's structure has been built. When you change one of your core beliefs you are seeing a new "truth" about the way things are for you. That flash of enlightenment is like the lightning hitting the tower. It starts off a whole chain reaction. The important thing about the Tower is its impact. A seemingly small or simple change gets things started—the result is much more far-reaching and complex.

Positive: You can see that by changing one basic attitude, opinion, or belief, you can really affect your whole life. Eventually, this one change will lead to a complete readjustment of your belief system or philosophy of life. You had some old, encrusted beliefs and attitudes that needed to be shaken loose. It's positive for you to see a new "truth" right now.

Negative: It's not time to be changing your beliefs and opinions: your beliefs remain valid for you. You may have some good, self-protective reasons for believing in certain things. Your basic attitudes are not really the problem. Examining your core beliefs will only create more confusion and turmoil.

Upright: You are in the process of changing a key and basic belief about the world. You have felt that certain things were true about other people or the external world and now you're examining one of those truths. You know that if you stop believing it's true, your whole picture of reality will be affected.

Reversed: You have held certain beliefs about yourself, but now you

97

are changing one of them. You may have always felt that a particular thing was basically and fundamentally true about you. You know that if you change that impression and accept the new idea, you will experience far-reaching ramifications in the rest of your life.

THE STAR - XVII

The Star is frequently represented by a naked person, usually a woman, dipping water from a lake or pond and pouring it back into the water or onto the ground. The stars are lighting up the sky, bright as day— they may even be sending little sparks or showers of light down to her. She looks as though she's surrounded by beauty, abundance, and the energy of nature and the Universe. She is taking the energy and pouring it out again with the assurance that it is infinite.

Neutral: You are experiencing the boundless, free abundance of the Universe. A flow of pure energy is available to you, in the form of resources that can be used for many purposes. You know that you have these infinite resources at your disposal. You can channel this energy wherever you want.

Positive: You are welcoming a new flow of energy and resources into your life. You are experiencing a burst of confidence or a feeling that you can accomplish whatever you want to achieve. You have the power to do it. You can use the energy that is coming to you for any projects that are important to you.

Negative: You aren't ready to be a channel for new energy or resources at this time. You may be drawing a lot of force or power into your life, but it's short-circuiting there. You could feel frantic or overwhelmed by the energy coming into your life without knowing what to do with it. It may not be healthy or appropriate for you to be the recipient for this energy right now.

Upright: You are receiving support or resources from your real-world activities. You could be getting money, possessions, attention, or labor from an outside source. You are aware of the abundance in the world and open to receiving it.

Reversed: Unbounded psychological or psychic energy is flowing to you. You're feeling personally energized and filled with enthusiasm. There is a never-ending supply of this powerful resource within you. You can use it in any way you desire.

THE MOON - XVIII

The Moon is usually depicted as lighting up a path through potentially unfriendly territory. The Moon illuminates the path that leads out of the watery depths of the unconscious, past landmarks or boundaries represented by towers, and into open country. Dogs guard the path. By following the light of the Moon, a traveler could come out of the murky depths onto a clearly lighted way.

Neutral: You are being guided by your greater, or Universal, self. Some doors are opening for you and others are closing. You realize that you're getting symbolic messages, showing you the path you need to follow. While your goal may not be totally clear, you sense that if you can just stay on the road, avoiding your doubts, fears, and hesitations, you will be guided to your destination. Your guidance is appearing in an intuitive or symbolic form. The Moon shows that you're trusting something other than your logical mind to be your guide.

Positive: You're trusting your greater self to guide you and you're getting good results. As long as you stay tuned to the signals, your intuition will show you where you need to go.

Negative: You're expecting a thunderbolt or dramatic flash of intuition to be your guide. You're looking so hard for a symbol, sign, or omen that you aren't taking the practical, logical steps that you could take. You need to be thinking things out for yourself, not just depending on cosmic intervention or rescue. You're abdicating responsibility for taking control of your life and expecting something else to tell you what to do.

Upright: Your guidance is coming in the form of symbols all around you. Some real-world event, letter, message, person, or sign is showing you where you need to be going. You're looking around you for signals that will be coming from outside yourself.

Reversed: The Moon's guidance is coming from within you. You are listening to your dreams, meditations, hunches, or inner voice for illumination.

THE SUN - XIX

The Sun is often shown shining down on young children at play. There might be a single child, riding a horse, moving away from the walls that provided structure in the past. In all cases there is the expression of youth but not of vulnerability. The children are emerging from a period of being sheltered, protected, or instructed. Now they are confident and fearless, prepared for their life's journey.

Neutral: You are experiencing a time of rekindled enthusiasm. Just as each child recreates the species and symbolizes the process of rebirthing humanity, you are revitalizing something that has previously existed in your life. Nothing is being destroyed; you are not losing or leaving the past. You have learned a great deal from past experiences and now you're ready to make refinements and adjustments so that you can re-do something you've done before in a new and more effective manner.

Positive: You are re-directing your growth, using the knowledge, experience, and learning of the past cycle as a base. You are justified in having high hopes and expectations. Having truly learned the lessons of the past, you are able to use what you've learned effectively. Now, you can make adjustments in something you've tried before and know that the result will be much more satisfying and successful.

Negative: You're just doing the same old thing in a new disguise. You are doing what you've done before in a new form and that original thing wasn't particularly good for you. You may be fooling yourself by thinking that you've really made enough adjustments and learned from your past mistakes. Watch out, you're doing it again!

Upright: You're coming to a bend in the road of your lifestyle, job, relationship, or worldly activities. You aren't leaving the past activities, projects, or people behind—you do value them. You're just choosing to be involved with them in a somewhat different way. You're experiencing a rush of enthusiasm for doing things in this altered way. You might be remodelling your current house or establishing a new contract in your old relationship.

Reversed: You are making adjustments in your self, based on past experiences. You feel that you're basically fine the way you are—with a few minor changes. You may be discovering new ways of expressing old feelings or putting a new look on your present body. You don't want to give up the self you are, you just want to make some changes so that you'll be more effective as that self.

JUDGMENT - XX

The Judgment card shows some fanfare that is symbolizing a rite of passage. In many decks, heavenly trumpets are being blown to signal the passage of souls into heaven. There is usually the sense of passing from one phase of life into another, more mature, phase.

Neutral: You are experiencing the natural process of growth and maturation. The old phase in your life is ending, not because of pressure or difficulties but because you've matured through the passage of time. You've reached this phase, like reaching puberty or like a seed growing into a flower, because you're growing up. You may be celebrating your "coming of age" through a rite of passage or ritual.

Positive: You are experiencing the joy of having things mature at their natural pace. You know that you are moving into a new phase in your life and you're celebrating the transition. You can trust that this natural maturation process is working out well for you.

Negative: The things that are naturally growing and maturing are not to your advantage. You may feel like you want to slow things down or speed them up — the natural or normal progression of things is just not right for you. If you let things develop at their own pace and in their own style, you probably won't be pleased with the results.

Upright: The events of your life are going through a phase change or maturing at their own pace. Your relationship (or your wine or your child) has grown and matured and is now moving into a new age. Things have progressed naturally and now you can symbolize or ritualize the passage into the new phase.

Reversed: Your personal biological or psychological timing mechanisms are signalling a new phase in your life. You may be reaching puberty or getting gray hairs. You could be growing up on an emotional level. You're recognizing that you're experiencing a personal rite of passage.

THE WORLD - XXI

The World card shows a dancer, usually female, in the center of a ring or oval, looking out at all the options that are available in life. Many potentials are present and she has the freedom and power to step out and make a choice. The world is her oyster.

Neutral: Everything is available to you. You are at center stage in your life and you're aware that you can simply reach out and choose one of many options. You know that the choices are complex, you're aware of the multiple factors that you need to take into consideration, and you realize that you will be making the choice yourself.

Positive: You are aware of your many options and you're keeping them all open. Your ability to be open to all the alternatives is your strength right now. Another good resource is your consciousness that things are not simple: they are complex. You are living in the midst of complexity and that's to your advantage at the moment.

Negative: You have too many choices before you. The complexity of your life is overwhelming and it isn't going to do you any good to stay in the midst of the confusion. You are keeping too many options open when you should be simplifying things and narrowing your choices. Multiplicity is not to your advantage at the moment.

Upright: Many possibilities are available to you, out there in the real world. It's up to you to experience the multiplicity and complexity of things and eventually make some choices. You are totally free to choose among multiple options.

Reversed: You have numerous possibilities available within your own being. You can be many selves and experience many levels of reality. You may even move in and out of various lives and various realities — at your will. You are aware that the Universe is a complex place and you are experiencing its multiple dimensions within your own consciousness.

7

DESIGNING A LAYOUT

Now that you know what the cards mean, you'll want to use them
to answer your questions. When using the Tarot, you will define your
questions through the card layout pattern that you use: this is the map
of the reading you've decided to do. It is a diagrammed plan of the
way you will lay the cards on the table. Each card answers one of the
questions you are asking. The plan can be as simple as one card if your
question is brief and well-defined. It may be as complex as 15 or 20
cards if you're exploring a multi-faceted issue. In any case, it creates
a format through which you can explore the answers.

You have the options of designing a layout pattern yourself, choosing a pre-designed pattern, or adapting a pattern that someone else
has designed. Working with someone else's pattern is easy because it's
all set up for you; it requires less time and thought. However, someone
else's plan may not exactly hit the current question on the mark. In
that case, you will want to design a layout that is specific to the situation. In Chapter 9, you'll find some examples of pre-designed layout
patterns. In this chapter, I'll describe how to design your own layouts.

Since your layout is a map of your questions, you begin the layout
design process by identifying and exploring what you want to know.
Once you have raised and examined all the issues around the subject,
you arrange all those issues into some kind of order. That order is your

layout plan. The plan clearly informs the Universe about what you want to know. You are saying to yourself and to the Universe, "If I could only know this and this and this, I would understand what's going on and be able to make a clearer decision." You are telling your all-knowing unconscious what you want to know so that it can give you the information you request.

When making your plan, ask your readee questions such as:

What are you concerned about today?
What are you interested in exploring today?
Is there anything in particular on your mind?
What do you want to get out of this reading?
What would you like to know about this issue?
What would be helpful to know?
What would be interesting or useful to know?
Do you want to know what's happening on an external level or on a psychological or spiritual level?
What do you really want to know?

Brainstorm for awhile, naming all the things you want to discover about the issue at hand. Try to get to the bottom of it. Sometimes, the process of clarifying the question makes the whole situation much clearer. At any rate, the brainstorming will clarify the scope of the reading.

If, for example, you have broken your leg and you're pretty sure that there's some reason for the break, your brainstorming might lead to questions such as:

What role is this broken leg playing in my life?
What role is this broken leg playing in my partner's life?
What can I do to help it heal?
Why did I break my leg?
What am I getting out of having a broken leg?
What am I avoiding by having a broken leg?

As you can see from the questions above, I usually work with questions that begin with words such as what, why or how, rather than questions that can be answered by yes or no. Occasionally, you'll want to do quick, one-card, yes/no type readings. Guidelines for those are given in Chapter 9. But most of the time you'll want to explore an issue, open it up for examination, and get descriptive or complex answers to your questions. You'll get more understanding and depth out of the reading if you keep your questions open-ended.

Once you are clear on what you want to find out, put the questions in some kind of order. Throw out the redundant or less pertinent questions and arrange the remaining questions into some kind of sequence.

The broken leg questions might be organized as follows:

1. Why did I break my leg?
2. What am I getting out of having a broken leg?
3. What am I avoiding by having a broken leg?
4. What is my partner getting out of my having a broken leg?
5. What is my partner avoiding by my having a broken leg?
6. What can I do to help it heal?

In this case, some of the brainstorming questions were re-stated or left out. The role of the broken leg seemed to be covered by the statements on what the readee (and partner) was getting or avoiding as a result of it.

One man wanted to know what was going on with his primary relationship. This relationship was important to him and things were not going well. He and his partner seemed to be fighting a lot and hurting each other instead of supporting each other. Some of the things he wanted to know were:

How do I feel about myself in this relationship?
How do I feel about my partner?
What's going to happen to this relationship?
Will my partner move out?
How does my partner feel about me?
What needs of mine are not being met in the relationship as it stands now?

What needs of my partner's are not being met?
What's at the root of the problem?
What can I do to improve things?

We organized these questions as follows:

1. What's at the root of the problem?
2. What needs of mine are not being met?
3. What needs of my partner's are not being met?
4. How do I feel toward my partner?
5. How does my partner feel toward me?
6. What can I do to improve things?
7. What will probably happen?

Again, some of the original questions were revised or left out. The question "how do I feel about myself..." was left out. We decided to use that concern as the lead-in for another reading about his self-image. We also decided that the question about what would happen covered the question about whether his partner would move out.

One woman wanted to change jobs. She was frustrated because her current job seemed to offer no opportunities for advancement; she was looking for a new career direction. Some of the questions she asked were:

What should I do?
What will help me do it?
What would I be good at doing?
What's wrong with my current job?
Can I find a better job?
What do I want out of my job?
What's the best way to get what I want?

We reorganized the questions as follows:

1. What's wrong with my current job?
2. What's right with my current job?

107

3. What kind of work would I be good at doing?
4. What should I do to get the kind of job I want?
5. What could help me do it?
6. What could block me from doing it?
7. Where will it lead?

In this case, two questions were added when we were organizing the questions. In addition to finding out what was wrong with her job, it seemed important to find out what was right with her job so that we could see what she liked in a job. In addition to finding out what could help her take the next steps, it seemed important to find out what could block her from taking those steps. Instead of a simple yes/no to the question "Can I find a better job?" she realized that she wanted to know where her job exploration would lead. She already knew that she could find a better job if she made some effort toward that goal.

In most cases, your initial brainstorming will lead to a variety of questions and issues. When those questions are placed in order, some of the questions will be dropped and some will be changed. Other issues will come up that need to be addressed.

Once the final list of questions has been made, go over it with the readee to make sure that everything that seems relevant to the issue has been included. Reassure her that anything that comes up as a result of the reading can be addressed in further readings. But also reassure yourself that the plan is pretty complete for now.

Then it's time to actually write out a layout pattern. This can be done very simply by drawing rectangles or circles, representing cards, for each question asked. The main thing at this point will be deciding how many cards to lay out for each question. For example, you may feel that there is more than one need that isn't (or is) being met in a relationship, that there is more than one thing to do to pursue a new job, that there is more than one block to pursuing that direction, etc. Use feedback from the readee to determine which issues are of the greatest concern. Choose the number of cards for each question accordingly.

The last step in the design process is to number the layout positions. Follow the order in which you plan to lay out and read the cards. You can choose whatever order you want; some of my students number the cards from the bottom up and some number them from the top down. Just be sure to number them. Laying out the cards for a large reading can be confusing if the positions are not numbered.

The visual pattern of the layout can be varied according to your personal preference. Some people like linear patterns. Others like diamond shapes, circular shapes, or star shapes. Feel free to create a layout design that appeals to you both conceptually and esthetically. At this point, you have your guidelines; you know what you want to discover, and you have set up a clear plan for pursuing it.

SUMMARY OF HOW TO DESIGN A LAYOUT

1. Discuss/brainstorm what the person wants to know, in the form of questions or issues.

2. Organize what they want to know in a list of questions or issues.

3. Make adjustments to the questions/issues as needed, adding new ones or rewording what you have, until you and the readee both feel that you have the appropriate questions and issues identified.

4. Draw out a layout plan for addressing those issues and questions, deciding how many cards should be allotted for each one and deciding on a design shape that appeals to both of you.

5. Number the layout positions on your plan.

The following two layout plans are examples of what finished layouts look like. both of these layouts were designed for the reading about the job search. In the first layout, the focus is on the current job and its advantages and disadvantages. The second layout focuses more on the steps to be taken and the blocks and resources that would affect those steps. The same questions were being asked in each case; the emphasis changed when the number of cards per question was changed.

Key Factor

16

Where those steps
will probably lead

13   14   15

Blocks that would
hinder me from tak-
ing those steps

10   11   12

Resources that would
help me to take the
steps

7   8   9

The steps I should
take to get the job
I want

4   5   6

The kind of work I'd
be good at doing

3

1   2

What's wrong   What's right
with my job   with my job

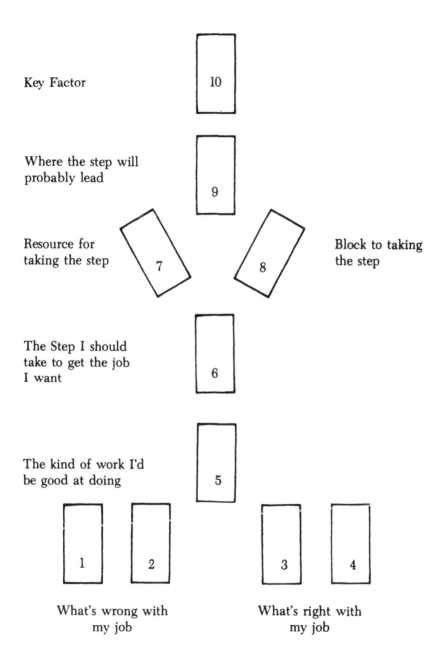

Key Factor

Where the step will
probably lead

Resource for
taking the step

Block to taking
the step

The Step I should
take to get the job
I want

The kind of work I'd
be good at doing

What's wrong with
my job

What's right with
my job

The following list gives you some suggestions for possible layout positions. It includes general issues and questions that can be applied to a variety of situations. Use them as a jumping off point for generating your own questions.

POSSIBLE LAYOUT POSITIONS

Significator
You
Who you are today
Another person
Conscious awareness
Subconscious awareness
Thoughts
Feelings
Verbal messages that are coming through
Non-Verbal messages that are coming through
Your point of view
Someone else's point of view
The basic nature of your relationship
The nature of your relationship in other lifetimes
The role you're playing in someone's life
The role someone's playing in your life
Things you hope for
Desired results
Things you fear
Feared results
Things you expect
Advantages of maintaining status quo
Disadvantages of maintaining status quo
Advantages of this course of action or choice
Disadvantages of this course of action or choice
What led up to this situation
The past
What this situation is based on
Situations in your other lives related to this one
Basic nature of this situation/relationship/etc.
Where this is likely to lead, short-term

Where this is likely to lead in the long run
The future
Your primary concern
The other person's primary concern
What you are doing to create this situation
What you are doing to create your desire
What you are actually getting out of this
What are some of the things you could do to change it
What are the next steps to take
What are the blocks/obstacles to taking this step
What are the resources/aids to taking this step
What you think you want
What you think you SHOULD want
What you really want
What other people want
What other people want you to want
The key factor
The main thing to keep in mind

Four of these layout positions deserve special note. They are the positions of the Significator, Another Person, The Key Factor, and The Future.

The Significator

Traditionally, in the Tarot, the first card laid out in a reading is called the Significator. It is a card, often chosen by the reader, that is supposed to represent the readee. Usually, it is one of the Court cards or one of the Major Arcana cards. This card is supposed to describe the person's personality and/or physical appearance.

Many Tarot readers today use specially chosen significators; there are also many readers who are choosing the top card off the deck or the first card drawn and having it be the significator. It is then interpreted as "the self you are today." The significator can give valuable information about the readee and her state of mind. It can help both the reader and the readee tune in to the readee's attitude, self- image, or personal position. It serves as a focal point for beginning the reading.

I use an actual significator card only occasionally. Instead, I find that most of the layout patterns I design include the person, her attitudes, and her self-image in them. Almost always, there is a card, somewhere in the reading that is labeled "the person you are right now" or "your attitude toward the situation" or "how you are feeling about this." I feel that these cards usually give the same information as a significator.

Another way of using a significator is for both you and the readee to draw a card at the beginning of the reading. The cards would show you how each of you is approaching the reading. The interaction between the cards can show your interaction with each other. The cards can also show the role you are each playing in the other's life. Are you an authority figure, teacher, therapist, priestess, friend, or parent to your readee? This kind of significator can show you.

I sometimes have my students design and color a blank card to show who they are today. This personalized significator is then used as the basis for readings. This process can be used with any readee. It gives a person a chance to draw how they feel if talking about it isn't easy for them. It also serves as a focusing device or ritual for tuning in to the reading.

Another Person

The Another Person position is rarely called "Another Person." Usually, it will be labeled something like "my mother,"" my boss," or even "my future partner." It can represent someone the readee knows or someone she has yet to meet. The person's basic personality can be described by the card placed in that position. The card may also describe the portion of the person's personality that affects the readee the most. Traditionally, Tarot readers have also used the cards to indicate the person's age, gender and physical appearance. These interpretations can be amazingly accurate. However, as I discussed in Chapter 1, most people are not represented in most Tarot decks. A "male" card such as a Knight might indicate a woman who is focusing her energy while a "female" card, such as the Empress, may represent a man who is a nurturer. Personally, I feel more comfortable describing personality characteristics than in getting too tied to the literal images on the card.

Key Factor

In most of my readings, I use a Key Factor card. This is a card that focuses in on the center of the whole situation. It is the key to the reading but I rarely call it the Key Factor as that phrase can be jargony or confusing for a readee. I name and interpret it in slightly different ways depending on the situation. Some of the phrases I use for the Key Factor card are:

What you need to keep in mind is . . .
The main thing for you to remember is . . .
The most important thing to focus on is . . .
Advice regarding this situation is...

The Key Factor card usually ties in with other cards in the reading, helping to emphasize the most important parts of the reading. It also serves as a focus for me to use when summarizing the reading.

The Future

The Future positions such as "What will happen?" or "Where will this lead?" are important positions to understand. The future is always a probability. It is based on the current present and the choices and decisions the person makes. Because the person is always free to make those choices, the future can always be affected and changed. So, you are not telling your readee what WILL happen, you are telling her what is LIKELY to happen given the present situation. She then has the option of supporting that direction or creating a different future. I always preface my interpretations of a Future card with "as things stand now, the probability is that..."

Use all of these layout positions as triggers for your own work in designing layouts. It might be easier to begin by designing fairly simple layout patterns and expanding on them as questions are raised. You might simply ask a question and draw a card—that's the essence of a Tarot reading anyway! Investigate different possibilities and see what works for you. Gradually, you will develop your own style.

8

THE READING PROCESS

Now, let's look at how you put the whole reading together. No matter how thoroughly you understand the meanings of the cards, your reading can fall flat if you can't integrate your presentation into some kind of unified process. In this chapter, I'll share the process that I've used when approaching readings. In time, you'll find your own process but you may find it helpful to have a few guidelines at first.

Before you begin a reading, make sure that you and the readee have matching expectations about the duration and value of the reading. Clarify whether you're planning to spend 45 minutes or 3 hours together. Establish your rate of "exchange." With your first few readings, you may be exchanging their reading for your practice. Later on the trade may turn into a reading for a massage or a reading for a homemade dinner. As your reputation spreads and your readees no longer come from your circle of friends, you may need to decide on a fee. Whatever your level of professionalism, it never hurts to make sure that the energy exchange is defined. Remember that, in addition to your knowledge, your time, care, and attention are valuable. If you set clear boundaries with your first few readings you can save a lot of awkwardness later on.

Once the parameters are set, use of the cards begins with creating a comfortable environment for the reading. This means an environment that is physically comfortable; no one should be straining to see the cards or sitting in an awkward position. It may mean procuring a chair that is the right height for the readee or supplying plenty of pillows if she's sitting on the floor. It may mean placing her with her back to the wall or to a corner so that she feels protected. It probably means finding a space where there is no commotion, no wind to blow the cards away, and no animals or children running through the reading. It means choosing a surface (the floor, a table, a board) where the cards can be laid out. The surface should accommodate a fairly large reading in case you decide to work with a complex issue.

You will also want to establish an emotionally comfortable environment. Your readee may feel insecure or fearful about having a reading. She may need to be relaxed, reassured and placed in a calm, harmonious space that feels safe to her. You can do this by closing your eyes and meditating with her for a moment, by talking with her about the reading process, by giving her a welcoming hug, or by showing her in your eyes and your manner that you accept her and want her to feel at ease.

Privacy and confidentiality are two other factors that can help to establish emotional comfort. Most of your readees will prefer to have private readings. They may feel freer to discuss what's really on their minds and freer to react to your comments if they are alone with you. When a readee is feeling especially vulnerable about a sensitive issue, privacy can be the key that allows her to open up. Occasionally, one of your readees will request that others be present at the reading. In these situations, the group involvement can actually enhance the reading (see the section on group readings at the end of this chapter).

In both individual and group sessions, I make it clear that the issues being discussed will remain confidential with me. I feel that the content of a reading belongs to the readee. It is up to her to decide how and when she wants to share the information and insight that she's gained. After the issues of privacy and confidentiality have been resolved, the climate of the reading usually becomes more relaxed.

On a practical note, a tape recorder can contribute immeasurably to a reading. If your readee is busy taking notes, she may not be able to fully participate in the reading process. A tape recorder gives her a record of the reading which she can later review, transcribe, and/or share with others.

Once you have comfortably established yourself in the reading space, spend a little time discussing the purpose of the Tarot with the readee. Demystify it as much as possible so that she is not expecting the sky to fall in at the end of the reading. Also, emphasize that you will not be telling her what to do; she is not giving you power over her. You are helping her to understand her own values so that she can make excellent decisions for herself. She always has the choice; she always has the power in her own life.

Then, talk with her about the value of dialogue in the reading. Explain that you need as much feedback from her as possible. She would not go to a doctor and say "I hurt, doc, guess where?!" She would give her doctor some clues and information so that the doctor could suggest appropriate action. In the same way, the more information she gives you, the more relevant the reading will be. Explain to her that you would like her to participate as much as she feels comfortable. Tell her you want feedback about what you are saying. You want to know how she is reacting to your comments.

When you are both comfortable and have established a sense of flow and communication between you, begin to address the question at hand. Spend some time finding out just what your readee wants to explore in the reading. Discuss the issue as fully as possible. Try to get beneath all the little things down to the core of the matter. Find out about her major concerns. If she doesn't know what she wants to discuss, a simple layout of two or three cards may help her clarify what she wants to explore. You might ask the question "What are the key issues for us to explore today?" and have her draw a card at random from the deck. This gives you a starting point for your discussion. The readee may just want a general reading that covers "my life and where it's going."

In any case, once you know what the person wants to explore, you can choose the appropriate layout for the issue at hand. You may choose a layout that has already been designed by you or someone else. Or, you may design a layout specifically for the current situation. Chapter 7 described how to design layouts. Chapter 9 gives some sample layouts and reading plans.

After you have designed or chosen the layout, write it down, number the layout positions, and go over it once more with your readee. At this point, she can guarantee that it really covers what she wants to explore. Make adjustments in the plan, as needed, until you both feel good about the layout. This is important because clarifying the question and defining your expectations sets the stage for the whole reading. Choosing the layout cements the agreement between you and the readee as to what is to be explored in the reading. You have agreed that you want to discuss a given issue and you have clearly let your inner selves, and the Universe, know how you want to explore it.

Now, it's time to shuffle and cut the cards. The goal is to mix up the cards so that they appear in the appropriate order. The readee's unconscious self, through her autonomic nervous system, will mix them up just right so that the relevant cards do fall into place. The mixing can be done by any combination of shuffling, cutting, or stirring the cards on the table. Usually, this is done with the cards face down. When I read for someone else, I usually mix the cards first and have the readee mix them last. Other readers choose to mix the cards by themselves or to have only the readee mix the cards.

When the cards have been mixed up until they feel "done," they can be laid out in the layout pattern. I usually take the top card and place it in position 1 of the layout, second card in position 2, and so forth. It is possible, however, to draw cards at random from the stack or draw from the bottom of the stack. Just stick to one system in any given reading. The layout positions will be numbered according to the plan you have agreed upon. So, wherever you draw it from, place the first card in layout position 1, the next card in position 2, and so on.

Most of my students ask me how they should draw the cards off the deck. They want to know if they should flip them to the side or over the top as they pull them off the deck. My feeling is that you will find a way of drawing the cards that feels comfortable to you. Your way may even be to vary your draws by whatever feels intuitively right at the moment. Use your own judgment.

Now, you have a layout. Some cards will be Major Arcana cards, some will be Minor Arcana cards. Within the Minor Arcana, several suits may be represented or only one suit may appear. Some of the cards will be upright and some will be reversed on the layout surface. They will all be laid out in accordance with the plan that you and the readee have devised. Once you have the layout, you are ready to do the reading.

The following steps are ones that I use in doing readings. I don't use every step in every reading but I use most of the steps most of the time. You will find your own adaptations to my style and eventually discover your own unique way of doing readings.

THE READING

The reading can be divided into three parts: groundwork, analysis and synthesis. First, you will scan the reading and get yourself centered with it. You may or may not share all of this groundwork phase with your readee. Then, you'll analyze each card in its layout position. Finally, you'll you'll put it all together in a synthesis.

Groundwork

This phase of the reading can be done very quickly and is your way of taking a look at the whole picture in order to center in on it. You may choose to share your observations with your readee or you may make mental notes that you'll bring up later at appropriate points in the reading.

Begin your scan by looking at the overall balance between uprights and reversals. More upright cards indicate that the reading is focusing on events that are happening out there in the objective "real" world. More reversals would show that the reading is concerned with psychological processes, inner awareness, unclear or very personal issues. An even balance shows that some of the issues are subjective/private and others are objective/public.

Look at the overall balance between Major and Minor Arcana cards. This lets you know whether the reading is about Universal concepts (Major) or general life processes (Minor). The Major-Minor balance also gives you a measure of the weight of the reading. A reading that is loaded with Major Arcana cards will probably have a deeper impact on the readee's life. An abundance of Major cards shows that the readee is learning many intense life lessons while a Minor Arcana emphasis shows that she's more involved with assimilating and using what she's already learned.

Look at the overall balance between the suits. This shows you the life process that is the focus for the reading. Maybe the whole issue centers around an identity struggle (Wands) or a concern with security (Pentacles). Also, notice whether a given number (like Two) shows up repeatedly in the reading. This will show you that your readee is working with the concepts represented by that number in many areas of her life.

121

Notice the cards that stand out in the reading. Is there one card in the reading that seems to be focusing the entire thing, such as a single Major Arcana card in the center of the layout pattern?

Now, you have a general sense of what the reading is about. From here, you can go on to a more detailed analysis of the cards.

Analysis

When you analyze a card, first identify it. Note whether it is a Major or Minor card—that will give you a clue as to the card's weight in the reading. If it's a Minor card, notice its suit and number. Name the card and then call its core meaning into your mind. To your readee, you might say, "In general, the Four of Cups means that you're taking some action based on your feelings or unconscious awareness."

Once you have focused on the card's basic meaning, describe the variation indicated by the card's upright or reversed orientation. You could say, "Since it's reversed, the Four of Cups shows that you're acting on your intuitive perceptions or manifesting your psychic potential. You might also be acting out a secret or hidden relationship or feeling. Given your current awareness and experiences, what makes the most sense to you?"

After you have clearly identified what the card means, you can go on to explain whether the card is neutral, positive, or negative for the readee. The layout position will give you the strongest clue as to value. In answer to the question "What's my best step to take?" you could say, "The Four of Cups Reversed shows that taking action based on your intuition is a good thing to do. It's appropriate, now, for you to manifest your psychic ability in a more concrete or useful way."

Interpreting the card in its position is probably the most important, and sometimes the most difficult, part of the reading process. You will have carefully designed or chosen a layout so that certain questions or issues could be addressed. When you analyze a card, relative to the question asked, it's important to let the card give you a direct answer. The answer is not desiring, working for, avoiding, or resisting the card: the answer is the energy of the card itself. Interpret the card, straightforwardly, in its position.

If my question is "What's the best thing to do now?" and the answer is the Ten of Cups Upright, my best bet is to hold off on making any decisions about relationships or emotional issues. I'm not ready to take risks; taking things at my own pace is what's best for me. The Ten of Cups is not telling me that my resistance to risk-taking is a problem — it's telling me that the best thing to do is to avoid those risks.

REMEMBER, ALWAYS INTERPRET THE CARD, STRAIGHTFORWARDLY, IN ITS POSITION.

You can easily determine the appropriate value for the card by looking at its layout position. Positive positions are those labeled as advantages, best steps to take, best action, or supportive resources. When interpreting a card in one of these positions, you will always take the most constructive application of the card's meaning and use it. Because of its position, the card is assumed to be positive. If the best step to take is The Devil, it's appropriate and positive to set boundaries and establish limits.

Negative layout positions are those labeled as problems, blocks, obstacles, or worst steps to take. When interpreting cards in these positions, it's important to use the more problematic interpretations. A Queen of Pentacles appearing as a problem or a block may indicate that a person is overqualified for a job. It doesn't indicate that she needs more skill ... the skill and maturity she already has is the problem.

Most layout positions are neutral. They are labeled with phrases such as "The Future," or "What I'm getting out of this situation," "The basic nature of the situation," "My mother's opinion," or "The status of my divorce proceedings." When a layout position is neutral, you can use your own sense of the situation to decide how to slant the card. Or, you can give the full stretch of the card. Show your readee some of the possible applications of the card's energy so that she can see that she has a choice in how to use it and will give you feedback on how she's experiencing it.

I was once doing a reading for a woman in which the Two of Cups Upright appeared in answer to the question "What's the best thing for me to do, right now?" I had seen her behaving affectionately with another person at a party, so I thought that the best thing for her to do was to claim or affirm a new relationship. Fortunately, I explained the basic meaning of the card and told her that she needed to be saying "yes" to new feelings and relationships. This was early in the reading and she was a shy person so she didn't give me too much feedback on the card. She seemed to understand what I was saying so I went on.

Halfway through the reading, she clicked into something I said and she released a flood of anger relating to her lover. By this time, she was feeling more comfortable with letting her feelings show but she felt a little guilty about the level of hostility she was feeling. At that point, I could go back and talk with her about the Two of Cups, explaining that it was important for her to claim and own her feelings. One way to work through her problems with her lover was to validate what she felt.

It turned out that the person at the party was an old friend—she was re-confirming that friendship. As is often the case, a single card may describe a process that's occurring in several areas of a person's life. In this situation, the most important thing for the readee to experience was her insight into her own angry feelings. By being open to her responses, I could interpret the card from the most effective angle.

In addition to the core meaning of the card, its orientation, and its value, you will want to use the added insight that you get from any symbols that appear on the card. Astrological symbols may clue you in to a specific emphasis; the colors may give you a certain feeling. The interaction between the people on the cards with each other, with nature, with buildings, with Cups, or with Swords may give you some more ideas. And, your intuition will give you some more clues. Listen to the ideas and impressions that pop into your mind for each card. Then, get feedback from your readee about each card and adjust your interpretation until you both agree on the significance of the card, for her, in this reading.

Synthesis

After you have clearly interpreted each of the cards, you can begin to synthesize your interpretation of the reading as a whole. Start by connecting each card to the one before it and the one after it in the sequence. Talk about how one card builds on the last and leads to the next. The connections will be there in the reading for you to see. Connect each card to other cards around it. Talk about patterns that may be formed diagonally or linearly. Look at how each card relates to all the cards around it.

Notice any flow from the beginning to the end of the reading. Is there a flow of color changes or a pattern in the number sequences? Is there a flow from Major to Minor cards or vice versa. Does this issue seem to be developing in a certain pattern? Discuss the natural flow of the reading with the readee.

Using your intuition and gather together all the strands of the reading. Explain the feeling that you get from specific cards and from the reading as a whole. Always get feedback from your readee as to the validity of your insights. But, trust your intuitive flashes to help you blend the elements of the reading into a whole.

Summarize the reading, talking about the whole picture, its flow, and its focus. End up with a statement that briefly expresses the intent of the reading. Your synopsis will put the whole reading into context and perspective for the readee. After you have completed the reading, always ask your readee if she has any questions. Answer them as best you can, given the information in the reading.

A question may arise from the first reading that is best answered by doing another reading. If you have time and the person is interested, you can now take any part of the reading that seems confusing or interesting and explore it in a new reading. For example, if the Tower appears in a prominent position, you may wish to do a reading on the nature of the beliefs that need to be examined or changed. You may design an entire layout around that card and its significance for the readee. Take as much time as you can to bring the session to a satisfying point of closure and completion.

Most of my students ask "What happens if I do another reading right away? Will I get the same result?" In my experience, a second reading will never contradict the first reading. It may take a part of the first reading and expand on it. It may focus on a totally different aspect of the readee's life. Or, it may show a further development of the person's awareness. Sometimes the inner connections that the person makes with the first reading are so instant and so deep that when the second reading happens, the person is already in a new space with her awareness. Feel free to do as many readings in a row as you want. There is no rule that says you can only have a reading once a month or once a year. You'll know when you reach the satiation point.

125

SUMMARY OF THE READING PROCESS

1. Establish a comfortable environment
2. Discuss the purpose of the reading
3. Choose or design an appropriate layout pattern
4. Shuffle, cut, etc.
5. Lay the cards out in the layout pattern
6. Interpret the cards

    Groundwork: Upright/Reversal balance
                      Major/Minor balance
                      Suit balance
                      Number emphasis
                      Focus card(s)

    Analysis: Basic meaning of each card
                      Orientation of each card
                      Value of each card

    Synthesis: Cards in relation to each other
                      Flow from beginning to end
                      Intuitive sense
                      Summary;

7. Answer questions
8. Do further readings as necessary

READINGS FOR YOURSELF

While many traditional Tarot texts warn against doing readings for yourself, I have found that self-readings can be invaluable. They can help you tune in to your own processes and identify your choices and direction. When you are having difficulty getting distance on a very emotional or puzzling issue, a Tarot reading can give you a shot of instant perspective. On the occasions when you feel so confused that you can't even interpret the cards clearly, you may wish to have a friend read the cards for you. Whenever you're doing readings for yourself, follow the same process as you would with another readee.

GROUP READINGS

Most of the time, you'll be doing readings for yourself or another person but occasionally you'll end up reading the cards in a group setting. Before I do a group reading, I check out the general attitude of the group toward the Tarot. Any group reading needs to be done in an environment of trust. It is also important that some consensus has been reached as to using the Tarot and that one person is not railroading the whole group into using it.

I have found that trying to do a single layout or reading for a group of people can get a little confusing. Each individual has a slightly different attitude toward the group and toward the matter at hand, and the cards tend to show the lowest common denominator. This can be helpful in some cases—it tells you what the base-line is. In the few instances where I have done a single layout for a group, I have had each person shuffle the cards. Then, I shuffle the cards last in order to get some kind of cohesion among all the shuffles. When I interpret the reading, the cards describe what the group as a whole is concerned about and where the group as a whole is headed. The group is seen as an entity in itself, having needs, problems, and potential directions just like an individual person.

When a group (or partnership) wants a reading about themselves and their interaction, my preferred method is to do individual readings for each of the group members. We choose one layout pattern that addresses the concerns of the group; then we explore how each person is experiencing those concerns by doing individual readings using the same layout plan.

At the end, I summarize the group interaction that has been described by the readings. If one group member seems to be particularly in disagreement, part of my final summary might include a statement about the opposing views that seem to exist. I may indicate that the general consensus seems to be one thing but a few people have differing opinions.

Sometimes, a group of close friends, a therapy group, support group, or consciousness raising group will choose to have personal readings in a group environment. The people in these groups have been opening up to each other and they've developed a good trust level. They want personal, individual, readings but they want to share those readings with others in this special group. And, they want the feedback of those people for their readings.

For these readings, I do individual readings just as I would for any client. However, I encourage the group members to participate in each reading. Often, something that is not clear to the readee may be elucidated by one of her friends. The friend may say "remember when you had that dream about . . . this reminds me of that," or "this sounds like what you were saying about . . ." After someone has made a comment, I feel that it's important to go back to the readee and get her reaction. Ultimately, she has to decide whether or not the comment is valid for her. If it is valid, I use it as part of the reading. If the readee seems to reject the comment, I tend to let it go as well.

The most important thing to remember when you're doing a reading in a group setting is that it's okay for you to be the leader. You are the one who is focusing the reading. You are the one who is pulling the strands of information together into one woven piece. You are combining the insights of all the group members into a whole. It's up to you to take the comments of the group members, get feedback from the readee, and summarize the reading yourself.

READINGS FOR CHILDREN

When reading for young children, it seems to work best to do short readings. I try to use fewer than five cards and to limit my comments on each card to really basic issues. Children are amazingly good at applying Tarot concepts to their lives and will usually open up a good deal once things get going.

It seems to help when I ask them questions like "does it feel like . . . to you?" or "are you having a problem with . . . right now?" I often do a simple three card (i.e. Past, Present, Future) reading to begin with and follow it up with questions and issues of concern to them. They tend to have questions that can be answered in two or three card layouts, designed on the spot.

With children, the issues of privacy and confidentiality seem especially important. They can become embarassed if other children or their parents are present. Taking them seriously enough to see them privately raises their trust level.

READINGS FOR SKEPTICS

Skeptics are another story altogether! The main thing that seems important when reading for a skeptic is to avoid taking a defensive posture. Stay firm with what you believe and trust in your own integrity. If you allow a skeptic to place you in a position of having to "prove it works" you're opening the door to a long debate and plenty of confrontation. You will have to keep proving it to her satisfaction. And who can say what will be satisfying to that person! Remember that the skeptic's acceptance or lack of acceptance of the Tarot is not the issue. The Tarot's validity does not depend on her approval. You aren't a good person because she accepts the Tarot and you aren't a bad person because she thinks it's hogwash.

If the skeptic is serious enough in her interest to want a reading, treat the request seriously. The strongest skeptics are often those who are most afraid of readings and most sure that their power and free will are being usurped by the reader or the cards. Sometimes, a little reassurance, some privacy, and a discussion about her freedom is enough to satisfy the skeptic.

Go through the reading process, as you would with anyone, calmly and confidently. Acknowledge her comments and questions, deal with her as seriously as you can without being challenged by her. Try to keep the flow of communication as open as possible.

If she is determined to challenge every card and unable to find any way of relating to the cards, let the reading go. Simply tell her that it's clear that you disagree about the value and purpose of the Tarot and that it's okay to disagree. You have no investment in making her agree with you. You have no investment in proving it to her. It works for you. You are not out to convert others, only to share with those who are interested.

The few unsatisfactory readings I've done have been for people who were dragged into it by a friend or partner. The readees really had no interest in the process and were there to go through the motions to satisfy someone else. In this situation, I try to be as thorough as I can in explaining what it's about. Then, I proceed with the reading as usual.

Whatever the situation, remember that every reading is an opportunity for tuning in to yourself, to another person, and to the patterns of the Universe. You will learn something from every reading that you do. My feeling is that, when I do a reading, all the pieces of the Universe and the fragments of my life make sense again. I can see the wholes that unite the divisions and I get a sense of centeredness and peace out of it. I am taking a ride in a hot air balloon, for myself or for another, and sharing what I see. Even readings that involve traumatic issues, imbue me with a sense of order and understanding. It is my hope that my clients also go away with a sense of order and, most important, a feeling of personal power. I want them to recognize that there are choices available to them and that they can solve their problems creatively.

A NOTE ON RITUALS

At this point, I would like to briefly address the subject of Tarot rituals. The purpose of a rituals is to help us focus on the issue or task at hand. Over the years, various people have discovered that certain action patterns help them to focus on the Tarot cards. They have systemized those patterns into rituals. Some of the most common rituals are:

Keep your cards in a pine box
Wrap your cards in silk (or cotton)
Sleep with your cards under your pillow
Never let anyone else touch your cards
Lay all your readings out on a pine board
Always face East when doing a reading
Light a candle (or incense) for a reading
Always face your readee
Shuffle and cut three times to the left
Shuffle once and cut three times
Don't shuffle, cut once to the right
Have only the readee shuffle
Have only the reader shuffle

As you may have noticed, I have not specified, at any time, how many times to shuffle, which direction to face when reading, or how to store your cards. This is because I feel that these rituals are very personal.

The rituals that I use are unique ones that developed themselves through years of habit. My favorite ritual is that, after laying out the cards, I am most compulsive about placing the remainder of the cards in their box or in a rubber band, or wherever I store that particular deck. And, I always shuffle first and have the readee shuffle after me. I have over fifty decks of Tarot cards and use five or ten of them in readings. I always give the readee a choice about which deck to use, usually a choice out of two or three decks. I don't mind if anyone handles my cards. I usually sit next to the readee so that the cards face the same way for both of us. I orient myself in the room, based on my comfort and hers.

If you like rituals, use them. If you have developed a habit, like holding the remaining cards in your hand after dealing out the layout, and that habit seems to help you focus, use it. No ritual is especially sacred. Its value is that it helps you to focus on the reading. The most powerful rituals are often those we invent ourselves. Use whatever rituals feel right for you when working with the Tarot.

9

WAYS TO USE THE CARDS

The only limit to the ways the Tarot can be used is your own imagination. Each life event, each emotional interaction, each inner awareness, presents us with an opportunity to understand ourselves and our Universe better. Every new problem or question is a challenge; with each challenge we discover new ways of using the Tarot.

This chapter contains some ideas on how to use the cards. Some of these ideas arose out of needs that were expressed by students or clients. When I asked what they wanted to explore, those people gave me an answer I wasn't expecting. They challenged me to find ways of working with their concerns. In my own life, issues of relationships, feelings, spiritual growth, political awareness, and personal development have all been triggers for finding new ways of using the Tarot. Some of the new ways turned out to be one-time layouts, appropriate only for specific situations. Other ways turned out to be general approaches or systems that could be used over and over again. See how some of them work for you.

QUICK FOCUS

The quick focus process was born when I was looking for ways to teach the difference between the Major and Minor Arcana. I used it as a classroom exercise and find it to be equally valuable as a reading process.

Divide the Tarot deck into two piles—the Major Arcana and the Minor Arcana. Choose a topic for your quick focus. For me, it's often "What's happening with me today?" or "What should I focus on today?" Sometimes it's a more specific issue like "What's the problem in our relationship?" or "What's blocking me from writing this book?!" After you've chosen your quick focus question, shuffle each of the piles separately. Draw one card from the Major Arcana pile and one from the Minor Arcana pile. Sometimes I take the top card from each pile and sometimes I take cards at random from the centers of the piles.

The Major Arcana card tells you the Universal Concept that you're working with in your life, in terms of the question at hand. It shows you that you're learning about regeneration and transformation (Death), limitations and structure (Devil), or cooperation (Lovers).

The Minor Arcana card shows you the best mode for doing that learning. It shows you if you need to be ending old relationships (King of Cups), acting on your ideas and thoughts (Four of Swords), challenging your old security patterns (Five of Pentacles), taking risks with your identity (Page of Wands), and so forth.

This reading tells you what you're learning from a specific situation and the best way to focus on it. I've found that the reading can be used quite effectively for a lead-off with people who aren't sure what they want to focus on. It gives us a direction for designing a longer layout that will thoroughly explore the issue.

DREAM WORK

One of the most exciting uses of the Tarot came to me through one of my students. When it came to be her turn to have a reading in class, she mentioned a recurring dream that she'd had for a number of years. She wanted to explore it. I asked her to recount the dream to us. As she described it, there were clearly discernable symbols and sections in it. For our brainstorming process, we simply recorded the parts of the dream, the significant images, people, and situations. Then we drew one card for each event or symbol in the dream. The result was astounding. She really had a break-through in her understanding of that dream.

Since that time, I've analyzed many dreams using the Tarot. For example, a client had a very short dream in which she was sitting on a riverbank, fishing. She got a bite but when she pulled it in, it turned out to be an old shoe. The elements of the dream and the cards pulled for each dream symbol follow:

> self — Two of Wands Reversed
> riverbank — The Hermit Upright
> fishing — Page of Swords Reversed
> bite — The Empress Reversed
> old shoe — Ten of Wands Reversed

We interpreted the dream by rephrasing it using the Tarot card meanings. We deduced that she was affirming a new sense of herself (Two of Wands Reversed) by retreating from the world and giving herself some privacy, confident that she had all the knowledge she needed to provide herself with insight (The Hermit). During the retreat, she took some risks with her life philosophy by daring to commit to certain values and beliefs (Page of Swords Reversed). She found that the retreat was nurturing of her self and her belief system (The Empress Reversed). While feeling nurtured, she did come upon some insight which let her know that her current self-image was stagnating and that it was indeed time to make some choices about the ways she wanted to name herself. However, it was also appropriate for her to take her time in making the choices, allowing herself to move slowly (Ten of Wands Reversed) into affirming that new sense of self-worth (Two of Wands Reversed). Our discussion of the dream was, of course, more detailed than this description, but this can give you an idea of how to begin when interpreting dreams.

DREAMWORK PROCESS

1. Break the dream down into recognizable parts, symbols, images, sequences, or events.

2. List the parts or design a layout using those significant dream events.

3. Lay out a card to show who the "I" is in the dream.

4. Lay out a card that shows the overall message of the dream for you.

For a long dream, you may wish to reshuffle after each section of the dream, allowing each of the cards to surface more than once. As in a regular reading, more than one card can be used for each dream symbol or event. However, I usually find that dreams are full of so many symbols that just one card per symbol leads to a sufficiently long reading. When I work with a dream, I use my own sense of the dream, its puns, its relevance to my life, and my own intuitive insights in addition to the information I get from the Tarot. But the Tarot information has consistently broken through blocks in my understanding of dreams and reduced the time it takes to get to the core meaning of a dream.

DIALOGUE

This reading process arose out of my interaction with friends and lovers. When working out a problem with someone else, it helps to have a common language, a tool that you can both use for communicating. As my closest friends have learned how to use the Tarot, we find that it can work well as a communication device.

Sometimes, we design layout patterns and do full readings to understand what's happening between us. Usually, those readings go off into more mini-readings as we get deeper and deeper into the issue.

Eventually, the dialogue process evolves.

We spread the cards face down on the reading surface. As we discuss the situation at hand, we draw cards to help us describe what we are feeling or thinking. When we can't get clear about what's going on, we ask "What's blocking our communication?" and each of us draws a card to show how we're blocking the flow. Or when one of us isn't clear on how to describe her feelings, she'll ask, "What am I feeling now?" Fewer and fewer cards are drawn as our communication improves. Finally, the issue is resolved. Sometimes, we each draw one card at the end to see how we feel about the resolution of the problem.

If communication is very strained and people are finding it difficult to open up, you can simply take turns stating your position and drawing a card that reflects that position.

That process might evolve as follows:

This is where I am . . .
Well, this is where I am . . .
My response or reaction to that is . . .
This is how that makes me feel . . .
If that happens, I'll feel . . .
I'm afraid that will lead to . . .
I hope this will lead to . . .
What I really want to tell you is . . .
What I think you're really feeling is . . .
My real need is . . .

In addition to being effective in one-to-one situations, the dialogue process can be quite valuable in collective, cooperative, or other group situations. If all the group members are not familiar with the Tarot, a facilitator who is skilled can interpret the cards that are drawn. In my experience, it has worked better if the facilitator is not a member of the group—just so she can maintain an unbiased perspective!

The dialogue process can also be used at the end of any reading to tie up loose ends and clarify anything that is still unclear. The readee just asks each question and pulls one or two cards out of the deck. You and she interpret the card(s) together. She asks her next question. She responds to that with another question, and so forth. She ends up having a dialogue with herself through the cards.

YES/NO

Some people want quick yes/no answers to their questions. For years, I avoided this issue, feeling that people needed to make their own decisions instead of being given pat or simplistic answers. For questions involving the future, I was leary of becoming too predictive and not holding to my choice-centered philosophy. I felt that my role was to help them uncover the advantages and disadvantages of two or more options; their role was to make the final decision. I still feel that way.

However, sometimes a readee has explored an issue that has so many pros and cons attached to it that the process of understanding the choice has already taken days, months, or even years. The choice has been narrowed to "six of one, half dozen of the other." In this case, I feel that the person's unconscious must have all the facts. Her inner self is well aware of all the pros and cons of the situation. Then, I feel more comfortable about using a yes/no layout to get an answer to a question.

Sometimes, the issue is trivial, like which movie to go to, calling someone now or later, or having tofu or hamburger for dinner. In that case, I also feel comfortable using a yes/no spread for a quick decision.

And, occasionally, the person can discover what she really wants by doing a yes/no reading. After the card is drawn, but before she knows what it means, I ask "In your heart, what are you hoping, thinking, or fearing it will be?" Sometimes, I don't even need to look at the card; the person already knows the answer.

The yes/no process that I use with the Tarot is only one process; other readers have developed other processes. You can develop your own process, simply by deciding which card will indicate what answer. You can decide that uprights are yes and reversals are no, or whatever. You can also roll some dice or spin a game spinner (odds are yes, evens are no). A pendulum can give you a quick yes/no type answer as well. Whatever you use, remember that the tool is giving you a predictive answer based on the odds at the moment. In my opinion, the answer should be preceded with a statement like "As things stand now, the odds are yes (or no)."

So with all due caution, here is the yes/no process that I use. I have found that it works pretty well for me. One of my students found that it worked exactly in reverse for her.

137

Minor Arcana: ODDS - YES
EVENS - NO
PAGE - YES
KNIGHT - NO
QUEEN - YES
KING - NO

Major Arcana: YES, if you want to put energy into working with the concept of the card.

NO, if you don't want to work with the concept of the card

Upright: If YES, definitely YES
If NO, definitely NO

Reversed: If YES, lay the foundation now for later; it may not seem like yes now but, after a delay, it will be yes

If NO, it may not seem like no now, but it will eventually be no; there is a delay here, too

TIMING

Because the future changes, depending on our choices and decisions, few readings can reveal a rigid, fixed interpretation of when something will happen. I find that questions about timing are the least accurate in my work with the Tarot. As in the case of layout positions that deal with the future and yes/no issues, interpretations of timing cards should always be accompanied with a statement like "As things look now, the timing looks like this . . . if you make new decisions tomorrow, based on this reading or other events, you may change the timing of these events."

For the question that is phrased "When will this happen?" or "When should I do this?" I draw one card from the deck. The key to that card is as follows:

Minor Arcana Cards: Upright

WANDS: Spring
Ace: week beginning with Spring Equinox
Two: week after Spring Equinox
Three: week after that
AND SO ON
King: matter was already completed last Spring

CUPS: Summer
Ace: week beginning with Summer Solstice
Two: week after Summer Solstice
AND SO ON
King: matter was completed last Summer

SWORDS: Fall
Ace: week beginning with Fall Equinox
Two: week after Fall Equinox
AND SO ON
King: matter was completed last Fall

PENTACLES: Winter
Ace: week beginning with Winter Solstice
Two: week after Winter Solstice
AND SO ON
King: matter was completed last Winter

Major Arcana Cards: Upright

If a Major Arcana card is drawn, the matter is close to being brought to a head or resolved. The timing depends on the person's psychological willingness to put energy into the process. The probable timing for the event is the number of days indicated by the Major Arcana number. The Fool indicates less than one day; the Empress shows that the event will probably occur in three days. The key here is not the timing but the person's involvement.

REVERSALS IN A TIMING READING

In a timing situation, any reversed card shows that the timing is particularly unpredictable. More information is needed, much is yet unclear. Too many things are up in the air for an accurate reading to be made.

ANOTHER TIMING PROCESS

Another kind of timing question arises when a readee wants to know where to focus her energy for the next week, month, or year. The reading process here, again, gives the probable direction of her focus. A one day or one week reading seems to be most accurate in terms of real events. The month or year reading tends to show the psychological process that will be at work during that time. How the person will be working with that process is pretty open.

The layout for this reading is fairly simple. Just draw one or two cards for each day, week, or month in question and lay them out in a sequence. This will show you the probable pattern for the time ahead.

This process can nicely show the flow of activity that is indicated for the period of time in question. It also shows what has to happen before something else can happen, indicating an orderly unfolding of growth and events. Once you understand the sequence, it's possible to speed the timing up by putting a lot of energy into it.

This kind of reading can be a help in deciding when to plan a vacation or other activity, depending on what kind of energy you want to use at that time. If you are planning to move, the Five of Pentacles may show the best month; if it's a scary move, it may be the Page. Or it may be that only one month out of the year shows any Pentacles at all. The Ten of Pentacles may indicate that you won't move after all. The decision to postpone the move will probably be made that month.

PRE-DESIGNED LAYOUT PATTERNS

I have included only a few layout patterns in this book because I believe you will find that the layouts that are best for you are in your own imagination. However, samples can sometimes get you going in your own creative process, so here are some examples. The first few are short ones that are easy to use as you begin your work with the Tarot. There are also some general life patterns, including one that I designed, the traditional Celtic Cross pattern, and my adaptation of the traditional Horoscope layout. I have given a layout pattern that is helpful in clarifying options when a person has a choice to make. And finally, a pattern for a person who wants to see the environment surrounding a choice she has already made.

Use these layouts, create your own, and let me know about other ways you've found to use the Tarot cards.

What's Happening Now?

1 - the nature of your present situation
2 - your attitude toward the situation
3 - the main thing for you to keep in mind

This layout is a quick way to focus on a particular situation. Its purpose is to clarify what's happening and to give insight into another perspective on the situation.

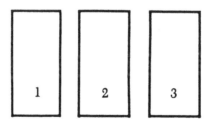

Past-Present-Future

1 - past, as you remember it
2 - present, as it stands now
3 - future, as it will probably unfold

This is a simple layout pattern that focuses on linear time.

It shows how the present is connected to the past and the future. It is most effective if a specific question is asked, like "what is the nature of my relationship with my father?"

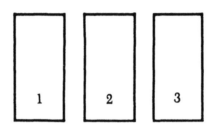

Six-Card Focus

1 - the role you play in the current situation
2 - the true nature of the current situation
3 - what led up to this situation
4 - how the situation is affecting you
5 - where this situation is likely to lead
6 - Key Factor

This layout pattern gives a basic picture of the person and the situation she's in. It gives a few more details about the situation than either of the three-card layouts.

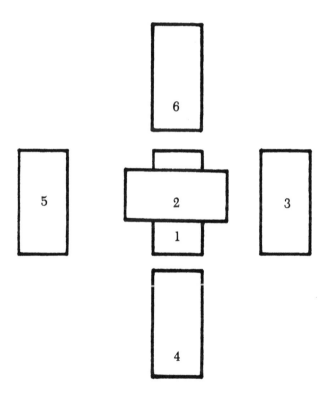

General Life Conditions

1 - Who you are right now
2 - How people and the environment are affecting you
3 - How your inner guidance is affecting you
4 - Something you value or believe in
5 - What you're thinking about
6 - What you're feeling
7 - The situation you're in
8 - Immediate outcome or short term result
9 - The long term outcome
10 - The Key Factor

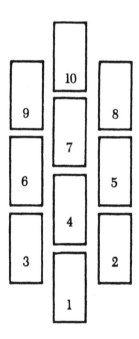

Celtic Cross (Traditional)

1 - The Significator
2 - What covers the person; current situation
3 - What crosses the person; what fate sends; something that is affecting the situation
4 - What crowns the person; conscious awareness; what's at the forefront of the person's mind
5 - What is beneath the person; unconscious awareness; what's hidden in the person's awareness
6 - What is behind the person; the past; an influence that is leaving the person's life
7 - What is before the person; the future; the probable direction in which the situation will develop
8 - The person in relation to her future; the strengths or weaknesses she brings to the future; how the person is creating that future
9 - Family and Friends; how the people around the person feel about that future; how they will affect that future
10 - Hopes and Fears; what the person fears or hopes will result out of that future; sometimes what we fear is the same thing as what we desire
11 - What will come; the probable long-term result or outcome of that future

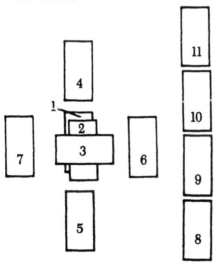

The Horoscope

1 - the self you are projecting to others; your appearance
2 - your money and possessions; your skills and talents; your values and self-worth; your earning power
3 - your mental or intellectual activities; your community or neighborhood involvement; short trips; siblings; school
4 - your emotional security or sense of belongingness; the activities related to your home; your mother
5 - your creativity and artistic ability; your children; love affairs and romance; recreation and leisure; gambling
6 - your daily routine; your health; your job or work; your co-workers; your tenants; pets; service activities
7 - your business partner(s); your clients; your primary relationship(s) or "significant other(s)"
8 - money or possessions belonging to the partnership; loans, grants, inheritances, taxes; transformative experiences; conception; death and rebirth; intimacy and sexuality
9 - your higher education; training opportunities; long-distance traveling; religion and philosophy; advertizing
10 - your public reputation; your contribution to society your career activities; your father
11 - your goals, dreams, and wishes; futuristic visions; friends, groups, clubs, and organizations; politics
12 - your spiritual situation; your psychic ability; your need for "retreats" from the world; escape and other fantasies

The following layout positions correspond to the twelve houses of an astrological chart.

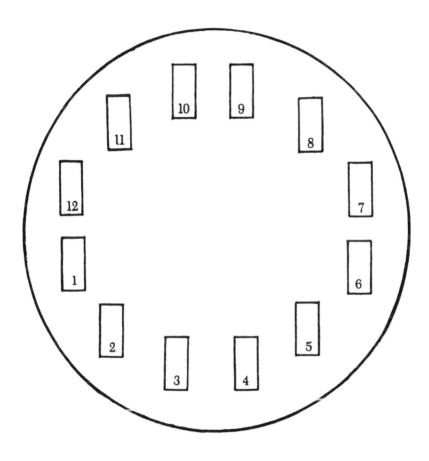

Clarifying Options

1 - your reason for considering this option
2 - what this option represents for you
3 - the true nature of this option
4 - the resources that support this option
5 - the obstacles that block this option
6 - the advantages of pursuing this option
7 - the disadvantages of pursuing this option
8 - what will probably happen if you choose this option
9 - the Key Factor with regard to this option

When a decision is necessary, you can lay out this pattern for each of the choices and options that the readee has defined. You may want to lay the cards out again for an option that she hasn't thought of yet. Card 3 will tell you about the nature of this option.

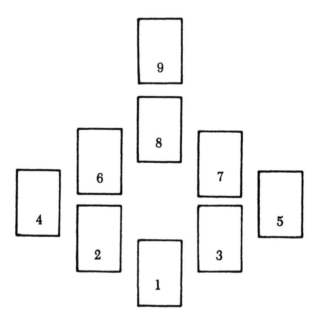

Important Step

1 - how you feel about this step; your underlying state of mind with regard to it
2 - the precipitating event that led you to finally take this step
3 - the effect that others will have on you as you take this step
4 - the effect you will have on yourself as you take this step
5 - your main worry with regard to this step
6 - what you hope to get out of taking this step
7 - what will probably happen as a result of taking this step
8 - the Key Factor

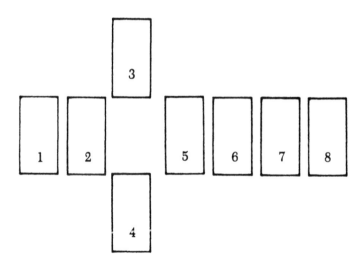

10

EXPANDING YOUR SKILLS

Now that you've read about some of my ideas, what's next? First of all, start practicing. The tarot itself is the best teacher around. The more you work with the cards, the more you'll understand them. The more you understand them, the more you'll come to know your own little quirks and trust your intuition.

One process that I used when first working with the Tarot was to start a Tarot notebook. I had two major sections in my notebook: Philosophy and Interpretation. Whenever I read, dreamt, intuited, or thought of anything philosophical that seemed related to the Tarot, I wrote about it in the philosophy section of my notebook. Gradually, I discovered that the ideas in this section transformed my own philosophy and that the Tarot (strangely enough!) mirrored the resulting philosophy.

For the interpretation section, I simply labeled one or two pages for each of the seventy-eight cards. Then whenever I got a new insight about a card, I wrote it on the appropriate page. Some of my insights came from other books, some from dreams, and some from readings. Gradually, I found and developed core meanings for each card. Eventually, I abandoned my other Tarot books in favor of my own notebook. That was the beginning of this book, of teaching classes, and of reading cards professionally. I still have my Tarot notebook, but most of my new ideas, now, go directly into a pigeon-hole in my head. The important thing is that I continue to learn and grow.

You'll keep learning, too. You may wish to set up a Tarot notebook of your own. Or, you may want to jot your ideas in the margins of this book. You'll probably want to keep a record of your readings—especially the ones you do for yourself. When you look back on old readings, you'll be amazed at how much your understanding of the cards has grown. You'll also be delighted by the accuracy of your early perceptions.

In addition to developing your interpretations for the cards, you may want to play around with Tarot card designs. Your own images and symbols are probably more powerful for you than any others. Experiment with doodling them out on 3 by 5 cards. Over a period of time, the images will probably evolve and coalesce. Then, you can buy a blank Tarot deck and reproduce your drawings onto the cards. Use your own symbols, colors, and titles. It will truly be your deck. If you are hesitant about your artistic ability, you can choose to have someone else draw out what you have designed. Many of the well-known Tarot decks were imagined by one person and actually drawn out by a more artistic friend. But don't underrate your ability. You may find that your style is just right for your deck.

Whatever you do with the Tarot, enjoy the process. The Tarot is one of the best celebrations around!

INDEX

Gail Fairfield was born in China and raised in Japan by missionary parents who encouraged her to discover her own answers to life's questions. Her college studies in Psychology and Education began to give her some clues about people and philosophy; but it was while teaching grade school that she got in touch with her own best teacher - her intuition. She was intuitively drawn to the Tarot in 1973 when a friend of a friend did a few quick readings for her. Over time, using that intuition as well as her practical experience, she developed her choice centered orientation to the Tarot - and to life.

Currently, Gail works out of her office in Bloomington, Indiana, doing personal and business consultations. She also teaches classes and workshops, both locally and out of town. If you're interested in scheduling a private consultation or atttending a seminar with Gail, please contact her directly:

P.O. Box 8661; Bloomington, IN 47407-8661
Phone: (812) 331-0501
email: gailfair@kiva.net
Web site: www.GailFairfield.com